CY TWOMBLY

CY TWOMBLY

FIFTY YEARS OF WORKS ON PAPER

Curated by Julie Sylvester
With essays by Simon Schama
and Roland Barthes

SCHIRMER/MOSEL
THE MENIL COLLECTION
HOUSTON

FOREWORD

By the time the Whitney Museum of American Art first exhibited the work of Cy Twombly in the *1967 Annual Exhibition*, Twombly had more than a decade of work behind him. Perhaps this delay was due to the fact that the artist had moved to Italy in 1957 as much as that the Museum had its sights trained elsewhere. But there was no avoiding his aggressively elegant, heartrendingly beautiful works once regular exhibitions of his art began at the Leo Castelli Gallery in 1960.

It was two years after his debut in the Annual when *Untitled* (1969), a major painting and one of the great treasures of the Whitney's permanent collection, was purchased thanks to Rudolph and Hannelore Schulhof. Twombly was subsequently included in three more Annuals/Biennials in the 1960s and 1970s, and his work has been shown in no fewer than thirty other Whitney exhibitions up to the present. The most significant was his first one-artist museum exhibition in New York in 1979, a survey of more than two decades of paintings and drawings. The exhibition, curated by David Whitney, was accompanied by a catalogue with a now classic text by Roland Barthes.

Today the Whitney is fortunate to have acquired another painting, *Untitled* (1964/1984), as a promised gift from our beloved, longtime trustee Emily Fisher Landau, two sculptures through the generosity of the Whitney's chairman, Leonard A. Lauder, and the American Contemporary Art Foundation, as well as several drawings and prints. Three monotypes—*Lepanto I*, *Lepanto II*, and *Lepanto III*—were published by Julie Sylvester to inaugurate Whitney Museum of American Art Editions in 1996.

It is in fact thanks to Julie Sylvester, associate curator of contemporary art at the State Hermitage Museum, that this exhibition was organized and the Whitney was able to host it. Sylvester curated this exquisite exhibition, which was not originally scheduled to be shown in the United States. When this was brought to our attention by our former trustee Fiona Donovan, we immediately inquired if we could secure the exhibition for the Whitney. The Museum is deeply grateful—as will be all the visitors who view the exhibition—to Sylvester and Twombly for extending the tour. Sylvester has been an enthusiastic collaborator and a great friend to the Whitney. Her knowledge of, appreciation for, and commitment to the art of Twombly is missionary in its intensity.

I deeply appreciate the efforts of the Whitney staff in bringing this endeavor to fruition. In particular, Dana Miller, Associate Curator, coordinated all aspects of the exhibition installation; Christy Putnam, Associate Director for Exhibitions, addressed all the logistical needs; Mark Steigelman, Manager, Design and Construction, assisted in the design of the installation; and Rachel de W. Wixom, Head of Publications, worked closely with Sylvester to reconceive and republish the current volume. Donna De Salvo, Associate Director for Programs and Curator, Permanent Collection; Arianne Gelardin, Publications Assistant; Jennifer Goldstein, Curatorial Assistant; Thea Hetzner, Associate Editor; Joelle LaFerrara, Assistant Registrar; Raina Lampkins-Fielder, Associate Director, Helena Rubinstein Chair for Education; Jennifer MacNair, Associate Editor; Carol Mancusi-Ungaro, Associate Director for Conservation and Research; Carolyn Padwa, Manager of Touring Exhibitions; Suzanne Quigley, Head Registrar; Jan Rothschild, Associate Director for Communications and Marketing; and Makiko Ushiba, Manager, Graphic Design, also contributed their talents to the Whitney's presentation of the exhibition. I also appreciate the support and involvement of my colleague Josef Helfenstein, Director of the Menil Collection, whose institution has made an extraordinary commitment to Twombly's art through amassing an unsurpassed collection of his work and establishing, in collaboration with the Dia Center for the Arts and the artist, the Cy Twombly Gallery. I would also like to acknowledge the cooperation of Deborah Velders, Head of Exhibitions and Public Programs at the Menil Collection.

Just as all exhibitions start with the artist, it seems that most acknowledgments end with the artist as well. We are honored by Cy Twombly's commitment to the Whitney. While he has resided outside the United States far longer than he has lived here, and has produced the lion's share of his art abroad, his career is proof that our conception of the American artist is mutable—the greatness of art knows no borders, and art itself is beyond definition.

Adam D. Weinberg
Alice Pratt Brown Director
Whitney Museum of American Art

Installation view of
Cy Twombly at the Hermitage,
The State Hermitage Museum,
St. Petersburg, 2003.
Photograph by Andrea Stappert

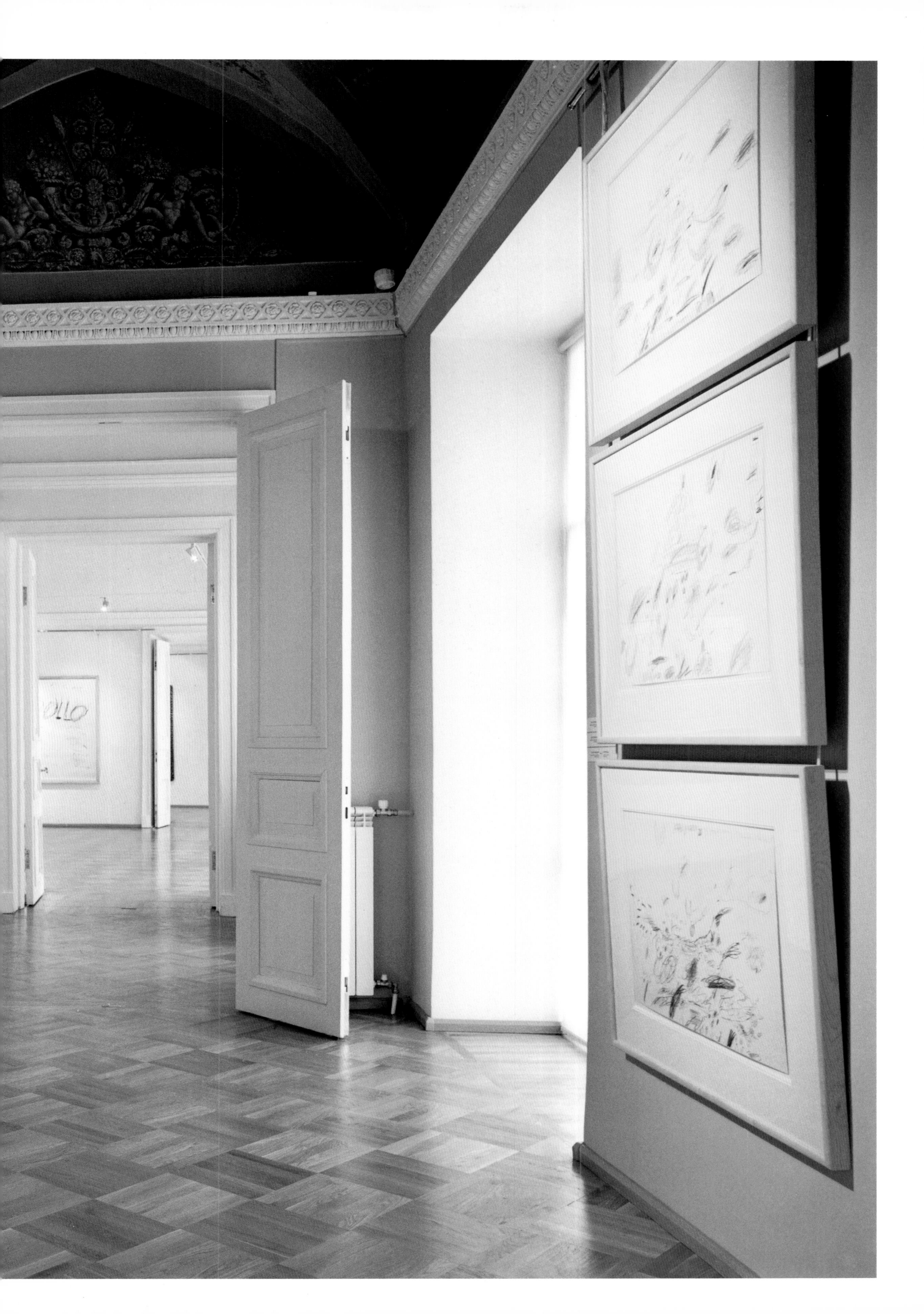

CY TWOMBLY AT THE HERMITAGE

On the 300th anniversary of the founding of the city of St. Petersburg by Peter the Great, the State Hermitage Museum presented *Cy Twombly at the Hermitage*, an exhibition comprised of fifty years of drawings and paintings on paper by the great American artist. By honoring Cy Twombly, an artist who paints epics and writes lines of poetry on paintings, we celebrated also the heroes and gods, the poets and muses, the mythologies and histories which have provided inspiration for artists through the centuries. The eighty-four drawings in the exhibition represent a gathering of time in Cy Twombly's œuvre, a selection that resounded poignantly within the larger gathering of several thousands of years of art, the collection of the State Hermitage Museum.

Cy Twombly at the Hermitage could not have been imagined even a few years ago, in the twentieth century. For my artist friends in St. Petersburg, the exhibition was keenly awaited. Cy Twombly's work is perceived as fundamentally subjective, truthful, and uncompromising, qualities missing from the experience of painting in the last century in Russia. For the Russian audience, the aim of the exhibition was to provide a rich understanding of Twombly's contribution to art history. The exhibition reached far beyond that aim and our expectations. The record number of extremely thoughtful visitors for one of the first major exhibitions of contemporary art at the Hermitage has signified an impact and an influence that will be strongly felt in the next generations of Russian artists and thinkers.

The selection of drawings for the exhibition was made directly with Cy Twombly over the course of two years, a participation quite unusual for the artist, and one perhaps motivated by his interest in the culture and people of Russia and in the Hermitage. All of the drawings were collected from Twombly's studio and therefore many works had not been previously exhibited or published. My partner and collaborator on the exhibition has been my very dear friend, Nicola del Roscio, who opened the archive and provided the access to drawings seen by few, always with his happy spirit.

The luxury afforded by an exhibition of fifty years of drawings may enhance a few notions about Cy Twombly's vision. For me, the revelation is in Twombly's close and steady relation to nature. It takes only a look at the paintings on paper made in Bassano in the summer of 1987, fleeting moments swept up at hurricane speed, or at the renderings of the leaflike shapes which—as if irresistible—appear decade after decade, symbols of life. Twombly is an artist who loves to be submerged in nature and changing surroundings. The crash of rough ocean against rocks can be monumental. A sun that blares through thick morning haze with sensational fuchsias and oranges can be the start of a day whose recollection may later spill onto a white sculpture. Twombly's recent paintings are steeped in color which is not the color of paintings—it is color absorbed by a quiet and ardent observation of nature.

And there are the celebrations of history, heroes, artists, and poets, the rawness of moments past brought fully and passionately to life, to our present. The commanding stances of *Pan*, *Orpheus*, *Apollo*, and *Venus*, *Adonais* and the soulful voice of Shelley, the twirling, tripping dance of *Nimphidia*, all reach our senses through drawings in which words are balanced by the stain of paint. *"Awake a moment, mind dreams again, red roses, black-edged roses.... as long as you have breath, breathe your last into my mouth, breathing your soul in my heart, til I've sipped the sweetness of your poison...,"* verse unattributable to any known writer ancient or contemporary, untraceable. *Petals of Fire* is a masterpiece, profound and compelling in gesture and emotion.

How wonderful to have the opportunity to be back among friends at the Whitney, an institution with which Cy Twombly has many ties. Flora Miller Biddle, Fiona Donovan, Adam D. Weinberg, and I have wished that the Whitney would be the institution for presenting this retrospective of the drawings, and happily we have reached that moment. I am very grateful to Adam, who so enthusiastically embraced the exhibition on behalf of the New York audience, and to my colleagues at the Whitney who have worked with vigor to make the exhibition and the new publication possible. It is fortuitous that the exhibition will arrive at the Menil Collection in Houston on the occasion of the tenth anniversary of the Cy Twombly Gallery. I would like to thank Josef Helfenstein for his immediate enthusiasm for the exhibition and for the efforts necessary to combine the opening of the exhibition with the anniversary celebration. It will be my great pleasure to join another friend, Paul Winkler, former director of the Menil Collection, in the planning and the installation of *Cy Twombly: Fifty Years of Works on Paper*. We are all grateful to Cy Twombly for the continuation of the exhibition tour.

Cy Twombly is my hero and has been for a long time. I imagine that there are more than a few painters who know exactly what I mean by this. Generosity is the core of Cy's painting and the reason we are so stirred by its beauty.

Julie Sylvester
Associate Curator of Contemporary Art
The State Hermitage Museum

CY TWOMBLY

by *Simon Schama*

I have always thought "Twombly" ought to be (if it isn't already) a verb, as in *twombly: (vt.): to hover thoughtfully over a surface, tracing glyphs and graphs of mischievous suggestiveness, periodically touching down amidst discharges of passionate intensity.* Or, then again, perhaps a noun, as in *twombly (n.): A line with a mind of its own.*

Cy Twombly has always walked his own fine (but seldom straight) line, between impulse and calculation. Marked by the Abstract Expressionism which ruled his coming-of-age, he has never been content with its sovereignty of pure instinct. But nor has he ever had much time for the ontologies which insisted on the containment of art within the boundaries of its own material construction. Conceptualist solemnities have been, for Twombly, mere balls of wool to unravel with a wicked flick of his cats paw. So any attempt to bundle him into the ism of the day is generally confounded by the restive fecundity of his reinventions. Ostensibly flirting with Minimalism, he appropriated its rectangularities, not to make them coterminous with the work, but to tweak and ultimately engulf them with the light movement of his errant marks. Even more malapropos is the attempt to turn him into some sort of neoclassicist on the grounds that Poussin and Jacques-Louis David also made the journey to Rome. Piranesi might perhaps be more like it, since not only does Twombly seem to follow the serpentine Line of Beauty, but his Rome consists of the pleasure of ruins; the attack of weedy nature on the defaced wreckage of the classical tradition. Insofar as he limns antiquity it is not the hard-edged discipline of celestial geometry; but the deeper, darker, Dionysiac archaisms of an Arcadia where Eros and Thanatos are the closest of chums and where the spilling of blood and semen blossom into Bacchic horticulture.

He is, I suppose, some sort of impenitent Abstract Expressionist—and the debt to Pollock has at various times been both clear and readily acknowledged; not least in Twombly's sense that the essence of the work is the traced process of its own making. And yet no one could be less of a pure AbEx practitioner—in the sense of the overriding need to nail down, visually, a surge of temper—than Cy Twombly, who has always been after matter less evanescent and, for all its admission of personal preoccupation, less emotionally self-absorbed. That matter, famously, has been the history (even the prehistory) of human marks: from the most archaeologically primordial of scratches and incisions to the development of the rhythmic dexterities which would generate calligraphy, and then before they could be attached to meaning, would break up into the disrupted and disrupting raw natter of scribble, doodle, and scrawl. Before ever there was Palm Pilot and pen Twombly was palm-piloting his cursive inscriptions in the loopy freehand he celebrates as a kind of proto-calligraphy; drawing blind as he did as an army cryptologist, the hand moving with the lights out, a wily owl of Minerva.

Don't be deceived by the courtly gracefulness of the Virginian translated to Italy; the lightly worn erudition; the genteel touch of his botanizing. The truth is that Twombly, at various times in his long, prolific, and protean career, has often been something of a scrapper, not in the sense in which his persona has ever exuded the kind of tear-away grab-baggy ebullience of his old comrade, Rauschenberg, much less the hard-ass demon-father, Pollock. Rather, Twombly has always enjoyed tearing a strip off the tendency of abstract painting toward its own monumentalism (enshrined for instance in the temple-like vacancies of color-field stains). His was the trash-rooting, bricolage-rummaging, cut-and-paste, slash-and-smear moment; a dumpster-full of wiry, rusty ganglia; a wall raucous with hoodlum graffiti. Twombly's resistance to "finish"; even to the all-over, fused, and thickly melded texture of Pollock's abstractions; his courage in performing looser, more disarrayed traces, is especially apparent in the works on paper, where the dog-eared, the torn-away, the dimpled, crumpled, chewed-up, and grubby are all enthusiastically welcomed into the creative process. The working materials, too, are a Falstaff's army of the art-maker, at the farthest possible remove from anything conspiring to aesthetic mystique: 4H dime-store pencils, ballpoint pens, oil crayons, house paint.

The happy-scrappy quality was there from the beginning, but it was overlaid for a while by what would turn out to be an uncharacteristic straining for runic gravity; so that the earliest monotypes (1, 2) give the effect of being etched or densely worked like petroglyphs, and end up by being strangely sluggish in their motion, even when they do their best to sprout, playfully. Paul Klee, often taken to be an inspiration for these early paper games, was, in fact, not quite the right mentor. When Twombly reversed the effect—pencil drawing on light paper—some of this self-conscious prehistoricity disappears, only to be replaced, sometimes with a different kind of oddity; and one which would return often in Twombly's repertoire—arrangements of biomorphic protuberances, shot through with allusions to zoological illustration, which in (3) suggests an entomological cemetery of defunct nematodes.

It is with the color pencil drawings of 1954 (5, 6, 7) that Twombly hits his stride, and it is already a limber gait; the line off on a fantastic dance, whirling and looping; pulling the artist's hand behind it; the colors raveling through each other, still playfully eroticized, the darker greens writhing at the center like so many snakes on the head of Medusa, while paler reds shade blissfully away into the indeterminate edge. Bolts of energy shoot through the scribbly mass which are already not like anything else in Abstract Expressionism; a comer's reproach to the stately formalism of Kline or Tanguy. But even these exercises look prosaic beside the speedy whirl of pencil of 1956 (9, 10) when Twombly created a filigree of lines racing across the page, dissolving subject and ground, creating subtle scrims which manage to be somehow both veil and disclosure.

In 1957 Twombly moved to Italy and, for a moment, some of this hectic energy takes a siesta. On paper, at any rate, the artist seems to be breathing more deeply; the vessel of his creativity a little becalmed. His marks turn discreet, drifting weightlessly over creamily coagulate surfaces, punctuated with the occasional sexy smear. But they seem—for Twombly—a little too laid back, too fluidly legato for an artist whose strongest motion is punchy staccato.

In the early sixties, however—and through the decade—Twombly's creative energy erupts, turning out an extended series of untitled compositions in which pictograms and ideograms—many, but not exclusively, sexual—swim and seethe in a broth of jittery action (14–19). It's all rather Pre-Cambrian submarine; fidgety with semi-evolved polyps, tentacular or tubal; ovoid and spermy, jiggly with fleshy playfulness. (One imagines companionate deep divers like Joan Miró and Pieter Brueghel off doing their own thing among the waving anemones). The Flemish called such paintings "wimme-beelden" or swarming pictures; in which caricatural details and half-obscured figures bounce and bob in carnivalesque commotion, with only the barest concession to classical pictorial hierarchy. The twomblies muck around doing their own thing (since they are, it must be said, very often tits and dicks) but do so in the patrolling presence of forbiddingly rectangular emblems of the Artistic Verities (from Albertian windows to Minimalist boxes), which hang around like embarrassed schoolteachers in a chaotically raunchy playground. 1968 was, of course, the moment when, all across Europe, in the slogan of the anti-Gaullist students, "Imagination came to Power." A cooler reality set in shortly thereafter, but Twombly's graffiti walls, though they sometimes wear a more formal regard, the monitoring frames and boxes recurring in greater strength, still jabber on with good dirty fun, capturing something of the moment's up-yours atmospherics; bubbles of raw energy popping against Conceptualist asperities. The effect is to puncture the universalizing pretensions of hard-edge Minimalism, for Twombly's energies are all about local animation; the unpredictability of the wayward line.

Through the paper works of the late 1960s and early 1970s—while Twombly was redesigning the landscape around his house at Bassano in Teverina, near the Renaissance "Park of Monsters" at Bomarzo in northern Lazio—the tension between linearity and ebullient organicism stays unresolved. His creativity feeding off the dialogue, Twombly occasionally moves into more genuinely Minimalist mode; laying down collages of irregular Schwitterian bands of paper; or blocky boxes of filled graphite (25, 26). But even these more austere, diagrammatic compositions ultimately get attacked by looser lines. For at the same time as he seems to be making a more serious engagement with Minimalism, Twombly is also experimenting with free-flowing pages of "auto" or proto-calligraphy, loops, coils, and spirals falling rhythmically over the surface, reminiscent of cursive exercises prescribed in Renaissance manuals of handwriting (21). The atmospheric effect—for which the dread word *beautiful* seems not completely inappropriate—is essentially musical, reductively simple yet cumulatively mysterious, suggestive both of childhood and eternity.

Then, in the mid-seventies, there is another caesura; certainly not a trailing off of Twombly's prodigious output, but rather what seems to be like a moment of earned reflectiveness. The collages lose their hectic chatter and are replaced again with creamy surfaces, nicked, slit, scabby with half-applied paper fragments, or patterned with yoni-like emblems that glide repetitively over the page (31, 32).

But this proves to be a pause before another immense leap: into the expressive pantheism which has never left him. A 1975 collage (39) can be thought of as something of a statement of intent; in which an aptly scrawled *Pan* is crowned by two tenderly caressing leaves of chard (one crimson, one gold) as if laid gently over the brow of the goat-lord. Beneath, in a quasi-fecal smear, is the visceral reality of his rule: *Pan-Ic*. Welcome, in other words, to the mixed blessings of Twombly's Orphic Arcadia. He is, evidently, now responding to a different kind of graffiti: inscriptions laid and overlaid on the ruins of antiquity, so the shorthand script used to summon up the demiurges of Apollo, Venus, and the rest must necessarily be impolite; the rough hand of Dionysian energy. Twombly's Apollo is not the fine-limbed hunk of the Belvedere, but the pitiless flayer of Marsyas. But what Twombly draws from archaic mythology is its poetic emphasis on the consolations of metamorphosis; cruelty, rape, and death (your usual day at the office in Olympus) transformed into the irrepressible burgeoning of nature. So Twombly lines up—literally—some of the victims along with their alter egos in flora and fauna.

His art then undergoes transmutation along with the bodies of the sacrificed heroes and heroines; and blossoms into fantastic blooms of heady, intense color, applied (like the paintings of the eighties) in mimicry of mythic energy, delivered, either in raw gouts and squirts of pigment, flattened and smashed on the paper, or in a dervish-like whirl of brilliant oil stick, vortices turning in space, coming hard at the beholder (46, 47).

Exactly at the moment when Abstract Expressionism was decreed to have been played out, Twombly's gorgeous, florid bolts of color, flaring and imploding over the surface invested the genre with new life—as if Soutine's ghost had traded the butcher's apron for the florist's. There are, to be sure, the much noted nods in the direction of Monet's *Nymphaea*—and in a more general sense, both Impressionism and even perhaps the Symbolism of Odilon Redon are recognized—but Twombly's bouquet is anything but decorative or mechanically emblematic. It is instead an almost anachronistic jolt of the Turnerian sublime; a theater of natural passions played out with snaking darts of cobalt; dropped gobs of chrome yellow; thinned-out sunset smears of coraline and salmon; bunched-up corners of angry cobalt and black like an AbEx Hades giving Persephone her time's up warning; about as "ideal" a marriage as Twombly can drolly concede (53–60). The work is as Olympian as a Flemish world-landscape; as shot through with mortal introspection as a Giorgione picnic in a tenebrous storm; as organically congested as a bug's-eye view of the herbaceous border; micro and macro; lyric and pastoral.

They are never sentimental, these color-implosions, but lest they risk ingratiation, Twombly, in the late eighties and early nineties, slaps them around a bit, his strokes coarsening, reaching for the wide eyes and fearless fists of childhood, the farther he gets from it (68–70); occasionally adding mournful, oracular jottings. In one particular rendering, a gloomy memo to self ("this is no time for poetry") accompanies a mere slug-trail slather as though, on a bad morning, the unlikely crosspatch has finally stuck his boot through the cucumber frame.

And like his alter ego, Proteus, through whom he signs off on a regular basis, Twombly remains capable of infinite self-alteration. Of late, he has turned from natural history to epic; recovering themes of ominous voyages and heroic collisions, first essayed in *Fifty Days at Iliam*. His masterpiece in the genre has been *Lepanto*, twelve painted panels, as big as the great Breda battle series of prints produced by Jacques Callot three hundred and seventy years ago. As usual, Twombly's maximalist-historicist instincts have been engaged by a profound problem of translation; and one, moreover, which shows no sign of going away: how do we visually euphemize war? Against banal "rectifications" of Goya, we might want to set instead Twombly's take on the ancient ideograms of battle, where the plans of men find themselves, literally as well as metaphorically, at sea. The renderings of warships are childlike, but no more so than where they first appear in the inscriptions of the warrior imagination: in the fleet of William the Conqueror making, cartoonishly, for the white cliffs across the unfurled film strip space of the Bayeux Tapestry Channel; in friezes of Roman triremes paddling to hubris, officered by captains who ought to have known their Thucydides. These are games, Twombly hints, as he offers us a lethally empurpled *Naumachia* (74) —the mock naval battles enacted in flooded arenas for the amusement of Roman crowds. But they are games of death.

The panels of *Lepanto* sail along the wall in the shouting brilliance of high Renaissance heraldry, all vainglorious scarlets, crimsons, and gold, until, that is, they implode in flame. The works on paper achieved around the same time are, in both senses, more impacted, claustrophobic nightmares of exitless confusion (76, 79). Some of the same hot hues that flowered in the pantheist songs of nature now, as Ruskin wrote of his own Turner, *Slave Ship: Typhoon Coming On*, "encarnadine" the sea. Local shots of color leak and spurt as from the site of a deep laceration. The endorphin pump of carnage hemorrhages lifeblood, while the eye-scalding brilliance of spectacle continues to swim in the transfixed gaze. It is as terrible and as beautiful an obiter dictum as you could ask from art. Yet the good ship Twombly sails redoubtably on.

NON MULTA SED MULTUM

by Roland Barthes

to Yvon
to Kenaud and to William

Who is Cy Twombly (whom I've decided to call TW)? What does he do? What name can we give to what he does? Certain words suggest themselves spontaneously—words like "drawing," "graphism," "scribbling," "*gauche*," and "childlike"—but immediately afterward one runs into a problem: at one and the same time (and this is very strange) *these words are neither false nor satisfying.* On the one hand TW's work is perfectly coincident with its appearance, and one must have the courage to maintain that it is flat, but on the other hand—and this is the enigma—this appearance is far from coincident with the language that so much simplicity and innocence should arouse in us as we observe it. "Childlike." Will that really do for TW's work? Yes, why not? But only as an additional definition: as something more or something less or perhaps off to one side. One says that a canvas by TW is *this* or *that* but it's most likely something different that simply *starts* as this or that. In a word (an ambiguous word since it's both literal and metaphorical), TW's work is *displaced.* To scan TW's work with our eyes and lips means constantly to disabuse ourselves of *what it would seem to be.* His works don't require that we refute the words of culture (since man's spontaneity is his culture) but they do require that we displace these words, distance ourselves from them, and see them in a different light. TW forces us not to reject but rather—and this perhaps is more subversive—to traverse the aesthetic stereotype. In short he incites us to undertake the *task of dealing with our language;* the work involved in performing this task—which is *our* task—may even, perhaps, be the source of the value of a work of art.

WRITING

TW's œuvre—and others have said it before me—is a question of writing and that has something to do with calligraphy. The relationship, however, is a relationship of neither imitation nor inspiration. A painting by TW consists only of what one might call writing's *field of allusions*. (Allusion is a rhetorical figure characterized by the saying of one thing with the intention of being understood as having said another.) TW makes a reference to writing (just as he also frequently refers to culture through words like *Virgil* or *Sesostris*) and then goes off to somewhere else. Where? To some place, precisely, at a great remove from calligraphy, which is to say from writing that is well-formed, clearly drawn, reposed, and finely modeled—from what the seventeenth century called *la belle main*.

In his own particular way, TW tells us that the essence of writing is neither form nor usage but simply gesture—the gesture that produces it *by allowing it to happen:* a garble, almost a smudge, a negligence. We can reason this out through a comparison. What would be the essence of a pair of trousers (if it has one)? Certainly not that carefully prepared and rectilinear object found on the racks of department stores; rather the ball of cloth dropped on the floor by the negligent hand of a young boy when he undresses tired, lazy, and indifferent. The essence of an object has something to do with the way it turns into trash. It's not necessarily what remains after the object has been used, it's rather what is *thrown away* in use. And so it is with TW's writings. They are the fragments of an indolence, and this makes them extremely elegant; it's as though the only thing left after the strongly erotic act of writing were the languid fatigue of love: a garment cast aside into a corner of the page.

With TW, letters are the very opposite of letterings and are formed without application, but even so they're not really childish since a child applies himself, presses carefully, rounds things out, sticks out his tongue; it's hard work to adapt oneself to the code of the grown-ups. TW takes his distance from it, relaxes, lets things slide. His hand would seem to enter into a state of levitation. One would say that he writes his words *with his fingertips*, but not out of disgust or boredom but rather because of a sort of fantasy open to the memory of some dead culture capable of leaving nothing behind it except for the traces of a few words. Chateaubriand: "Urns engraved with indecipherable characters have been found on some of the islands of Norway. To whom did the ashes belong? The winds have no secrets to disclose." TW's writing is even emptier: it can be deciphered but not interpreted. Even though precise, the very traces may just as well be discontinuous. Their function is nothing other than to render that *vagueness* that prevented TW from becoming a good decipherer of military codes when he was in the army. ("I was a little too vague for that.") Vagueness, however, paradoxically, excludes the idea of enigma. Vagueness has nothing to do with death. Vagueness is alive.

Rather than the products, TW conserves the gesture of writing. Even though the results of his labors (what one calls "the work"or "the canvas") can be consumed aesthetically and even though the things he produces form a part of a History and a Theory of Art (and they could hardly do otherwise), what he shows us, visibly, is a gesture. And what is a gesture? Something on the order of the supplement to an act. An act is transitive; its sole purpose is to have an effect upon an object or to achieve a result. A gesture is the indetermined and inexhaustible sum of motives, pulsations, and lassitudes that surround the act with an *atmosphere* (in the astronomical sense of the term). We can distinguish between the *message*, which wants to produce information, the *sign*, which wants to produce intellection, and the *gesture*, which produces all the rest (the "supplement") without perhaps really wanting to produce anything at all. The artist (and let's keep this somewhat kitschy word a little while longer) is a performer of gestures by definition. He wants to produce an effect, but at the same time he couldn't care less. And the effects he produces are not necessarily effects that he wanted to produce; they are effects that have rebounded, spilled over, and escaped, effects that come back to him full circle and provoke modifications, deviations, and diminishments of their own traces. Gesture, in fact, abolishes the distinction between cause and effect, motivation and target, expression and persuasion. The gesture of the artist—or the artist as gesture—doesn't actually interrupt the causative chain of acts, what the Buddhists call *karma* (the artist is neither a saint nor an ascetic); it does though do something to garble the chain, to make it rebound to the point of finally losing its meaning. In Japanese Zen (and I am simplifying) one calls this brusque and sometimes tenuous rupture of our causal logic a *satori:* on account of some lowly, derisory, aberrant, or simply bizarre sort of circumstance the subject *awakens* to a radical negativity (which is more than simply a negation). I think of TW's "graphisms" as so many little *satori*. Starting out from writing (a field of causalities *par excellence* since one writes, one presumes, to communicate), a series of useless explosions that are not even the interpretations of letters manage to suspend the active nature of writing along with the tissue of its motivations, its aesthetic motivations as well: writing is nowhere and no longer to be found, it is absolutely *de trop*. And one wonders if it isn't at this extreme limit that one finds the true beginning of man's "art,""texts,"and everything else that is "useless"—his perversions, his excesses.

TW has been compared to Mallarmé, but the terms of the comparison—a sort of superior aestheticism that ought to unite them—are pertinent to neither the one nor the other. Attachment to language, as was the case with Mallarmé, implies having fixed one's sights more seriously—or more dangerously—than can ever be the case with aesthetics. Mallarmé's purpose was the deconstruction of the Sentence, the time-honored vehicle (in France) of ideology. TW's deconstruction of writing takes place *en passant*, just dragging along, as it were. And to deconstruct something is not at all equivalent to making it unrecognizable. In the texts of Mallarmé, the French language is fully recognizable and fully functional—to be sure, in bits and pieces. In TW's graphism, writing is likewise fully recognizable: it presents itself as writing. Nonetheless, the letters that are formed no longer belong to any graphic code, just as the grand phrases of Mallarmé no longer belong to any rhetorical code—not even to the code of destruction.

There is nothing written, then, on these surfaces of TW's and yet they would appear to be the receptacle of the entire universe of written things. Just as it's said that Chinese writing was born from the cracklings of an overheated tortoise shell, one could say that the writing in the work of TW is born from the very surface on which it comes to find itself. No surface, no matter what the distance from which one looks at it, is truly virginal. A surface is always and already asperate, discontinuous, uneven, and rhythmed by accidents: there's the grain of the paper, the smudges, the trellisings, the interlace of tracings, the diagrams, the words. At the end of this chain, writing loses all of its violence. What finally imposes itself is not this or that form of writing, nor indeed the essence of writing; it's rather the idea of a graphic structure. TW's work holds up a sign that says *"to be written"* just as one could imagine a sign that says *"take me"* or *"eat me."*

CULTURE

In TW's œuvre the germs of writing are sometimes of great rarity and at others they multiply into a frenzy. It's as though we were dealing with some sort of graphic itch. In tendency, then, writing becomes culture. When writing feels itself constrained, explodes, and pushes out toward its margins, it approaches the idea of the Book. The Book that is virtually present in TW's work is the Book as it used to be, the Book with notations: additional words invade the margins and the spaces between the lines and become a gloss. When TW writes and repeats the single word *Virgil*, that already constitutes a commentary on Virgil. The name, written as it is by hand, does more than simply call up the complex of an idea (moreover, an empty idea) of classical culture; it also functions as a reference—a reference to a time of unaccustomed studies, calm, purposeless, and discreetly decadent. English colleges, Latin verses, desks, notations in finely written pencil. This is what culture is for TW: an indulgence, a memory, an irony, a posture, the gesture of a dandy.

GAUCHE

It's been said that TW's work looks as though he did all of his drawing with his left hand—*avec la main gauche*. French is a right-handed language. Anything that vacillates in its movements or that can't keep a straight line or that is clumsy or embarrassed is generally called *gauche;* and even though the word *gauche* is a moral notion, a concept or a judgment, the French language has turned it into a physical and purely denominational term that has defenestrated the archaic word *sénestre* and that now simply means "left." *At the level of language*, the subjective has served as the basis for the objective. (One can observe the same thing in another corner of the language where a purely emotional metaphor gives its name to substances that are entirely physical: the lover enflamed, the *amado*, is paradoxically the source for the name applied to all inflammable substances, *amadou*). This essay into etymology is sufficient proof that by producing a series of written signs that seem *gauche* (or *gauchère:* left-handed), TW is deranging the morality of the body—and this is one of the most ancient forms of morality since what is "anomalous" is considered a deficiency and a deficiency is considered a fault. If his graphisms and compositions present themselves as *gauche*, that's tantamount to relegating TW to the circle of the excluded, the emarginated, where, to be sure, he is to find himself in the company of children and invalids. A *gauche* (or *gaucher:* someone left-handed) is somehow considered blind: he can't get his directions straight, can't understand the implications of his gestures; he is guided only by his hand, by the desires of his hand and not by its aptitude as an instrument.

The eye is reason, evidence, empiricism, verisimilitude, everything that serves to control, coordinate, and imitate; and as an art exclusively voted to vision, all of our painting of the past has found itself subjugated to the repression of rationality. TW, as it were, has liberated painting from vision: the *gauche* (the *gaucher*) destroys the connection between hand and eye. He draws in the dark (one of TW's habits in the army).

Unlike many of today's painters, TW shows us his gestures. We are not asked to view, think, or savor the product, but rather to review, to identify, and, one would even like to hazard, "to play" the movement that has taken place precisely *there*, in precisely that space. Ever since humanity has possessed the art of handwriting (we can leave the printing press aside), the trajectory of the hand and not the visual perception of its work has always been the fundamental act that allows letters to be defined, studied, and classified. In paleography, this finely ruled act is what's called the *ductus*. (The hand conducts its tracings from high to low, from left to right, by turning, by pressing, by halting, and so forth). And it's clear that *ductus* is of greatest importance when dealing with ideographic writing. Rigorously codified, it allows the classification of the characters according to the number and direction of the strokes of the pen and even creates the possibility of dictionaries for systems of writing that have no alphabet. *Ductus* is the very principle of TW's work: not the rules of *ductus*, but rather its games, its fantasy, its explorations, its indulgences. In short, it's a form of writing of which the only thing that remains is the slant and the cursiveness. In ancient writing, cursive was born from the necessity (the economic necessity) of writing quickly:

lifting the pen is expensive. Here it's exactly the contrary. Everything flows, and tumbles, showers like a fine rain or falls like grass—erasures made in indolence as though it were a question of giving a visibility to time, to the very tremor of time.

Many of these compositions—it's been said—resemble the scrawls of children. The child, the *enfant*, is the *infans:* the person who doesn't yet speak. But the child that guides TW's hand already knows how to write, has already become a little schoolboy: lined paper, colored pencils, rows of slanting bars, repeated letters, tiny clouds of shadings like the smoke that curls out of locomotives in children's drawings. But all the same, the stereotype (what things would seem to be) manages once again to return subtly to the scene. The production (the graphic production) of a child is never ideational. Entirely without mediation, it directly conjoins the objective mark of the instrument (that commercial object called a pencil) and our little student's *this* or *that* as he leans intent and insistent over his page. TW interposes idea between his instrument and his imagination; the colored pencil becomes color as pencil; reminiscence (of the schoolboy) becomes an all-inclusive sign—of time, of culture, of society (something that has less to do with Mallarmé than with Proust).

Gaucherie is very rarely light. To be *gauche* is most frequently to be a little pushy. True clumsiness is insistent, obstinate, and anxious to be liked (just as the child wants to *show* what he has done and exhibits it triumphantly to his mother). TW frequently demonstrates that he has the ability to reverse this contorted *gaucherie* that I'm talking about: his *gaucherie* doesn't push at all. Quite the contrary. It draws off bit by bit into the background and grows indistinct even though it manages to preserve the delicate smudge of a passage with an eraser. The hand had traced out something like a flower and then decided to scumble about with its tracings. The flower was written and then unwritten, but the two movements remain vaguely superimposed upon each other. It's some perverse sort of palimpsest. There are three texts (if one counts what would appear to be a signature, a legend, or a citation, the word *Sesostris*), each of which tends to efface the others, but for the sole purpose, one would imagine, of rendering the effacement legible—a true philosophy of time. As always, life (art, gesture, effort) must undespairingly bear witness to ineluctable dissolution. In generating themselves (like this chain of *a*s that grows out of a single and continuous circular movement of the hand, repeated and constantly displaced) and in rendering their generation legible (which used to be the purpose of the *sketch*), forms, or at least TW's forms, no longer sing so much of the marvel of generation as rather of the sad sterility of repetition. One could imagine them to have the task of creating some one single state capable of containing both what comes into being as well as what fades away. To separate the exaltation of life from the fear of death is flat and tasteless. Utopia (of which art may perhaps be the language and to which all human neurosis opposes resistance) would be to produce but one single feeling—neither Eros nor Thanatos, but Life-Death as a unified thought, as one sole gesture. Such a Utopia can be approached neither by violent art nor by cold art; it can rather be approached, to my taste, by TW's art—an art that remains unclassifiable since its inimitable tracings conjoin inscription and effacement, infancy and culture, drift and invention.

THE SUPPORT?

It would seem that TW is an "anti-colorist." But what is color? Joy. This joy is inside TW. To understand this, one has to remember that color is *also* an idea (a sensual idea). For color (in the joyous sense of the term) to be present, it's not at all necessary that it be confined to emphatic modes of existence; it's not at all necessary that it be intense, violent, rich, or even delicate, refined, or rare, nor indeed level, impastoed, fluid, etc. In short, it's not necessary that the color be affirmed or *installed*. It's sufficient that it simply appear, that it be there, that it prick up like a pin in the corner of an eye (a metaphor, in *A Thousand and One Nights*, that indicates the excellence of a story), that something be rent by it. It's enough that it pass before the eye like an apparition—or a disappearance—since color is like an eyelid that flutters, a momentary swoon. TW doesn't paint color; at most one could say that he colors. But his coloring is rare, interrupted, and always something alive, as though he were trying out his pencil. What we can read through these traces of color is never an effect (even less a verisimilitude), rather a gesture, the pleasure of a gesture—the vision of something that is born out of the tips of one's fingers, born out of one's eye, something both expected (I know, for example, that the pencil I am holding is blue) and unexpected (not only am I ignorant of precisely what blue will appear, but even if I weren't it would always still come as a surprise since color, like event, is new again every time it happens: this suddenness is what accounts for color, just as it accounts for joy).

What's more, there's no doubt that color is *already* present in the paper that TW uses since the paper is *already* dirtied or altered by some unclassifiable luminosity. Only a writer's paper is truly white or really "clean,"and that is far from being the least of his problems. (The difficulty of the white page can frequently cause a sort of panic about how to go about dirtying it.) The writer's great sadness (and this is what differentiates him from the painter, especially a painter of writing like TW) is that graffiti are forbidden to him. TW, in short, is a writer who's established a right of access to graffiti and who exercises his right in plain view of everyone. What's more, one knows very well that the essence of graffiti is to be found in neither the inscription nor the message. The essence of graffiti is the wall, the background, the tabletop. The background, the support, has a full existence of its own as an object that already has had a life of its own and this is why whatever is scribbled across it always comes as an enigmatic supplement. Order finds itself disturbed in the presence of something *de trop,* additional, out of place. Or again, insofar as the support is neither clean nor proper it becomes an impropriety for the reception of thought (unlike the white page of the philosopher) and thus the most proper thing of all for everything else (art, indolence, impulse, sensuality, irony, taste: everything that the intellect might choose to think of as so many little aesthetic catastrophes).

It's as though we were dealing with an extremely delicate surgical operation. With TW everything happens in that infinitesimal moment in which the wax of his crayon approaches the grain of the paper. The soft wax adheres to the fine asperities of the graphic field and the trace of this leavened flight of bees is what typifies the mark that TW leaves. This is a very singular form of adherence since it contradicts the very idea of adherence: it's like a caress whose value finally lies in the way it's remembered. But the *past* of TW's traces could also be seen as their future. The crayon, medium oily and only half-sharpened (one never knows the movements it will make) *is about* to touch the paper. Technically, TW's work seems to conjugate itself either in the past or the future tenses, and never truly in the present. One would say that there is never anything more than the remembrance or the harbinger of his traces. On the paper—and because of the paper—time is in a state of perpetual incertitude.

Let's consider the drawing of an architect or an engineer, the blueprint of a machine or a building. What we see has nothing to do with the materiality of a graphic sign; we are concerned with its "sense" and not with the performance of the technician who made it. In short we don't see anything, except perhaps a kind of intelligibility. And now we can descend to another level of graphic materials; when confronted with a piece of handwriting we are still again concerned with the intelligibility of the signs, but there are also other opaque and insignificant elements—or rather elements of a different significance—that capture our attention and what can already be called our desire: the nervous turn of the letters, the flow of the ink, the cast of the strokes, a whole series of accidents that are not necessary for the functioning of the graphic code and that are already, in consequence, a series of supplements. We can step still farther back from meaning: a classical drawing presents us with no preconstituted signs, and there is no longer the communication of any functional message. My desire is caught up in the rendition of the analogy, the success of the execution, the seduction of the style: in short, in the final stage of the product. What I am contemplating is truly an object. The chain runs from a blueprint to a drawing, and as we move along its length, meaning evaporates bit by bit in order to make room for another sort of ever more useless "profit," and TW is what we find at the end of it: there are signs, yes, but the signs have grown pale and *gauche* (as we've said before) as though the artist were entirely indifferent to the possibility of deciphering them; but above all, if one can say such a thing, there is the *final state* of painting, its support: the paper. ("TW insists that he has a greater sense of paper than of paint.") And yet, things come curiously full circle: since sense or meaning has been exhausted, and since the paper itself has become what one can justly call *the object of desire*, drawing can reappear once again, absolved of all technical, expressive, or aesthetic function. In some of TW's compositions one rediscovers the drawing of the architect, the craftsman, or the surveyor as though one freely returned to the origin of the chain to find it purified and liberated from all of the conditions that seemed for centuries to justify the graphic reproduction of objects that are *recognizable*.

THE BODY

A line—any line inscribed on a sheet of paper—is a denial of the importance of the body, the body and its flesh, the body and its humors. The line gives access neither to skin nor to membranes laden with mucous. It speaks of the body only insofar as it scratches and grates (one might even go so far as to speak of tickling). Line causes a displacement in art; no longer concerned with the object of desire (the lovely body sculpted in the marble), it turns its attention to the subject of that desire. Line, no matter how supple, light, or uncertain, always implies a force, a direction. It is *energon*, work, and it displays the traces of its pulsation and self-consumption. Line is action become visible.

TW's line is inimitable. (If you try to imitate it what you do will be neither his nor yours; it turns out to be simply *nothing*.) But the most fundamentally inimitable thing of all is the body. No discourse, either verbal or plastic—except perhaps for the discourse of anatomical science, which after all is fairly gross—can turn one body into another. TW's work makes this fatality visible. My body will never be your body. This fatality may lie at the root of certain human unhappinesses and there is only one way to get around it: seduction. The only solution is for my body (or its sensual substitutes, art and writing) to seduce, transport, or derange the body of another.

In our society, the very slightest graphic traces—since they issue from the certainty of the body and its inimitability—can be worth millions. What's consumed (since we live in a consumer society) is a body, an "individuality" (which is to say, that which, above all, cannot be divided). In other words, what one buys when one buys the work of an artist is in fact the body of the artist—we're dealing with an exchange in which we are forced to recognize a contract of prostitution. And one wonders if such a contract is typical only of capitalistic societies. One wonders if it furnishes a specific definition of the commercial mores of our own particular world of art—mores, moreover, that are often fairly shocking. In the People's Republic of China, I've seen the work of popular (rural) painters whose work, in principle, was entirely disconnected from any sort of exchange. But the situation also seemed to be a curious sort of wild-goose chase where two persons were trying to find each other and never managing to bring it off. The most lavishly praised painter was the author of a flat and correct composition (the portrait of the secretary of a party cell as he was reading) and there was nothing bodily in the sense of line (no passion, no indolence), nothing but the trace of an analogical operation (a good resemblance, with the subject looking expressive). At the other extreme, the exhibition abounded with other works in the style called "naïf"—works, even in spite of their realistic subject matter, that communicated the impassioned body of the amateur painter as it pressed outward, exploded, and indulged in its joys—a voluptuous roundness in the drawing, excitement in the colors, an intoxicating repetition of motifs. In other words, the body always escapes beyond the terms of the exchange in which it is involved. None of the commercial systems of the world and no set of political virtues can ever exhaust the body. There is always some extreme point at which the body gives itself *for nothing.*

A useful and fecund morning—in any case a pleasant morning. I slowly look through an album that reproduces the works of TW and I frequently stop to try my hand at rapid scribblings on small sheets of paper. I don't try directly to imitate TW (why should I?), I imitate the tracings that I infer, if not unconsciously at least dreamily, from my reading. I am copying not the product but rather the production. I try to place myself, if the expression is permissible, *into the stride of the hand.*

This in fact (for my body at least) is what TW's work is all about. It's a *production* delicately imprisoned or enchanted within that aesthetic product one calls a canvas or a drawing, and collections of which (in a book, an album, or an exhibition) are never more than anthologies of *traces.* TW's works oblige his readers (and I say *readers* even though there is nothing to decipher) to assume a certain philosophy of time. One must look at a movement in retrospect, observe an ancient becoming of the hand. But in that case, and this could be a salutary revolution, the product (perhaps all products?) would seem to be a kind of will-o'-the-wisp. All art, insofar as it is stored, delivered, and published, is declared to be *imaginary*. What is real—and this is what TW's signs and traces always call us back to—is the process of its production. With every stroke of his crayon, TW disrupts and destroys the Museum.

There is a kind of sign, entirely without abrasion or lesion, that I would hazard to call "sublime." The instrument that makes its trace (a pen or a pencil) descends toward a sheet of paper and simply lands—or "moons"—upon it, that's all. It doesn't even hint at biting in, it simply *comes to rest*. The almost oriental rarefaction of the slightly smudged surface (that is the *object*) is responded to by the extenuation of the movement. It grasps nothing, it finds its poise, and everything has been said.

If the distinction between product and production that I've proposed as the foundation of all of TW's œuvre seems sophistic, one might consider the decisive clarification that other terminological oppositions have been able to give to certain psychic activities that at first sight would seem confused. The English psychoanalyst D.W. Winnicott has clearly demonstrated that it is false to reduce the games of children to a purely ludic activity; he asks us to note the opposition between *game* (which is strictly ruled) and *play* (which is free). TW, to be sure, is involved with play and not with game. But that isn't everything. At a later stage of his discourse, Winnicott goes from *play*, which is still too limiting, to *playing*. The child's—as well as the artist's—reality lies in the process of manipulation and not in the product that's produced. (Winnicott then systematically replaces a series of concepts with the verbal forms that correspond to them: fantasying, dreaming, living, holding, etc.) All of this works very well for TW. His work is based not upon a concept (the *trace*) but rather upon an activity (*tracing*)—better still, perhaps, one could say that it's based upon a field (the sheet of paper), insofar as an activity takes place within it. According to Winnicott, children's games are less important than the atmosphere that surrounds them. For

TW, "the drawing" is of less importance than the atmosphere that drawings inhabit, mobilize, work on, and explore—or rarefy.

MORALITY

The artist has no morals, but he does have a *morality*. His work contains these questions: *Who are the others for me? How am I to desire them? How am I to accommodate their desire? How am I to behave among them?* Constantly enouncing a "subtle vision of the world" (the words of the *Book of Tao*) the artist *composes* what is allocated (or refused) by his culture and what comes with insistence from his own body: what is avoided or evoked and repeated, or better, what is forbidden and desired. This is the paradigm, like a pair of legs, that the artist stands on, *insofar as he produces*.

How does one go about drawing a line that isn't stupid? It's not enough to make it undulate a bit in order to give it a little life. As we've said, one has to be able to be *gauche* with it. Intelligence always has something a little *gauche* about it. Look at these two parallel lines that TW has drawn. They end up by meeting each other as though the artist hadn't been capable of insisting on the *maintenance* of the obstinate space between them that gives them their mathematical definition. What *seems* to intervene in TW's line and to lead it to the edge of that tremendously mysterious *dysgraphy* that constitutes the essence of his art is a certain indolence (which is one of the body's purest forms of expression). Indolence: this is what is permitted by "drawing" and prohibited by both "painting" (all finished and completed colors are violent) and writing (every word is born entire and full of will, armed with culture). TW's "indolence" (and I'm talking about an effect not about a disposition) is nonetheless a question of tactics: it allows him to avoid the platitudes of graphic codes without giving himself over to the conformism of destruction. In every sense of the word, it's a matter of *tact*.

This is something very rare: TW's work is entirely free of aggressiveness. (It's been observed that this is one of the things that differentiates TW from Paul Klee.) I think that I've discovered the reason for this effect, and it's an effect entirely contrary to all art in which there's an engagement with the body. TW seems to proceed in a way typical of certain Chinese painters who have to bring off the line, the form, and the figure in a single gesture and without being able to correct what they've done because of the fragility of the paper, of the silk. This is painting *alla prima*. TW would seem to trace out his graphisms *alla prima*. But whereas impulse forces the Chinese artist to run the great risk of "ruining" his figure by not striking the mark of his analogy, TW's line comports no risks at all. It has no goal, no model, no exigencies. It is free from *telos* and therefore free from risk. How could one "correct oneself" when there is no drawing master? It follows that any sort of aggressiveness would be somehow pointless.

The *value* that passes through TW and into his works can be aggregated to what Sade called *the principle of delicacy* ("I respect tastes and fantasies... I find them respectable... since even the most bizarre, once one has analyzed them as one should, always return to a principle of delicacy"). As a principle, "delicacy" is neither moral nor cultural; it's an impulse (and why should impulse always be defined as violent and coarse?), *a certain request of the body itself.*

Twenty-four Short Pieces. That has a resemblance to both Webern and Japanese haiku. And in all three cases, we're faced with a paradoxical art that might even be considered a "provocation" (if it weren't for its delicacy), an art whose concision plays against its profundity. In general, everything that is brief seems concentrated: rarity engenders density and density engenders enigma. But with TW a kind of drift occurs. To be sure, there is a silence, or, to be more precise, a fine and tenuous crackle of the page, but this background is a positive force in its own right. By reversing the usual relationships to be found in a classical drawing, one could say that it's the line, the grating, the form, in short the graphic event, that allows the sheet of paper to exist, to signify, to play. ("Being," says the *Book of Tao*, "offers possibilities, but it's through non-being that one makes use of them.") Number no longer has any pertinence to the space being dealt with, and yet that space never ceases to be plural. And one wonders if this scarcely tenable opposition that excludes both number and unity is not perhaps the guide to be followed in interpreting the dedication that Webern so precisely addressed to Alban Berg: *Non multa, sed multum.*

There are paintings that are excited, possessive, and dogmatic; they impose their products and attribute them the tyranny of a concept or the violence of avidity. TW's art—and here one finds its morality as well as its extreme historical singularity—*desires to take possession of nothing at all.* It hovers, floats, and drifts between desire, which is the force that subtly animates the artist's hand, and the polish of politeness, which is the discreet dismissal of every desire to capture or possess. If one wished to find a reference or a precedent for this morality, one would have to go and look for it at a considerable distance: well removed from painting, well removed from the Occident, well removed from historical consciousness, and at the limits of meaning. One would refer to the *Book of Tao*:

> He produces without appropriating,
> He acts and expects nothing,
> Having accomplished his work, he remains unattached,
> And since he is unattached,
> His work will remain.

Paris, 1976.
Roland Barthes
translation by Henry Martin

mfly

mitage

- 8-21 Sept

2003

PLATES

1. UNTITLED, 1953
Monotype in paint
18 7/8 x 25 3/16 in. (48 x 64 cm)

2. UNTITLED, 1953
Monotype in paint
18 7/8 x 25 3/16 in. (48 x 64 cm)

3. Untitled, 1953
Pencil
25 3/16 x 34 1/4 in. (64 x 87 cm)

4. Untitled, 1953
Pencil
25 3/16 x 34 1/4 in. (64 x 87 cm)

5. Untitled, 1954
Color pencil
19 1/16 x 25 3/16 in. (48.5 x 64 cm)

6. Untitled, 1954
Color pencil, crayon
19 1/16 x 25 3/16 in. (48.5 x 64 cm)

7. Untitled, 1954
Color pencil, crayon
19 1/16 x 25 3/16 in. (48.5 x 64 cm)

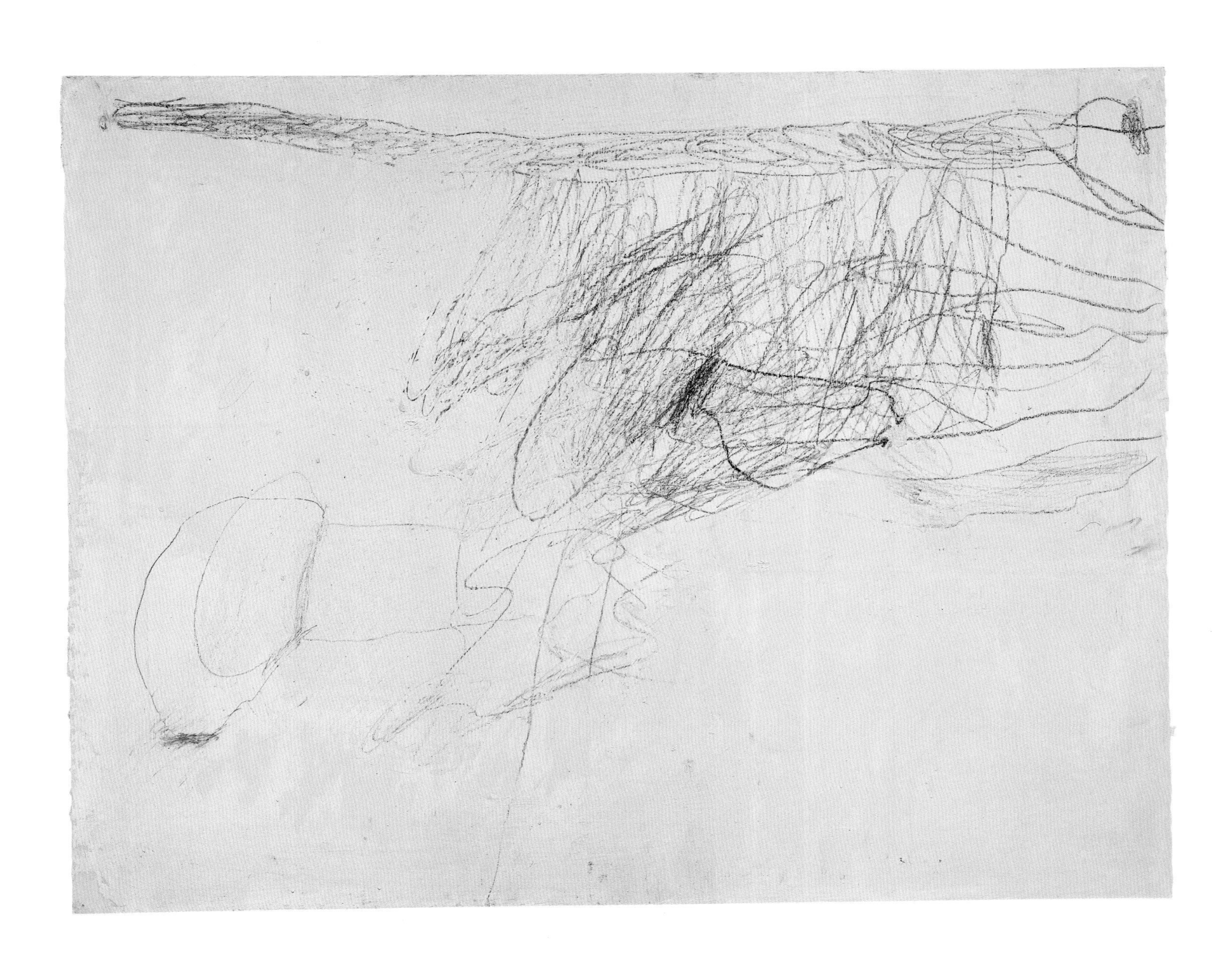

8. Untitled, 1954
Pencil, house paint
43¼ x 54¼ in. (110 x 138 cm)

9. Untitled, 1956
Pencil
22 x 30⅛ in. (56 x 76.5 cm)

10. Untitled, 1956
Pencil
22 x 30⅛ in. (56 x 76.5 cm)

11. Untitled, 1957
House paint, pencil, color paint
27 3/16 x 38 11/16 in. (69 x 98.3 cm)

12. UNTITLED, 1957
House paint, pencil, color paint
27 9/16 x 38 3/8 in. (70 x 100 cm)

13. Untitled, 1959
Collage, glue
$33\frac{1}{2}$ x $24\frac{3}{8}$ in. (85 x 62 cm)

14. UNTITLED, 1961/1963
Pencil, color pencil, ballpoint pen
19 11/16 x 28 in. (50 x 71 cm)

15. Untitled, 1961
Pencil, color pencil, ballpoint pen
19 $^{11}/_{16}$ x 27 $^{15}/_{16}$ in. (50 x 71 cm)

16. Bolsena, 1969
Pencil, color pencil, felt pen
57 1/4 x 71 1/16 in. (145.5 x 180.5 cm)

17. BOLSENA, 1969
Pencil, color pencil, felt pen
57 1/4 x 71 1/16 in. (145.5 x 180.5 cm)

18. Bolsena, 1969
Pencil, color pencil
27 9/16 x 39 3/8 in. (70 x 100 cm)

19. Bolsena, 1969
Pencil, color pencil
27 9/16 x 39 3/8 in. (70 x 100 cm)

20. Untitled, 1971
Wax crayon, house paint
27 3/4 x 39 3/8 in. (70.5 x 100 cm)

21. Untitled, 1970
Wax crayon, house paint
27 9/16 x 34 1/4 in. (70 x 87 cm)

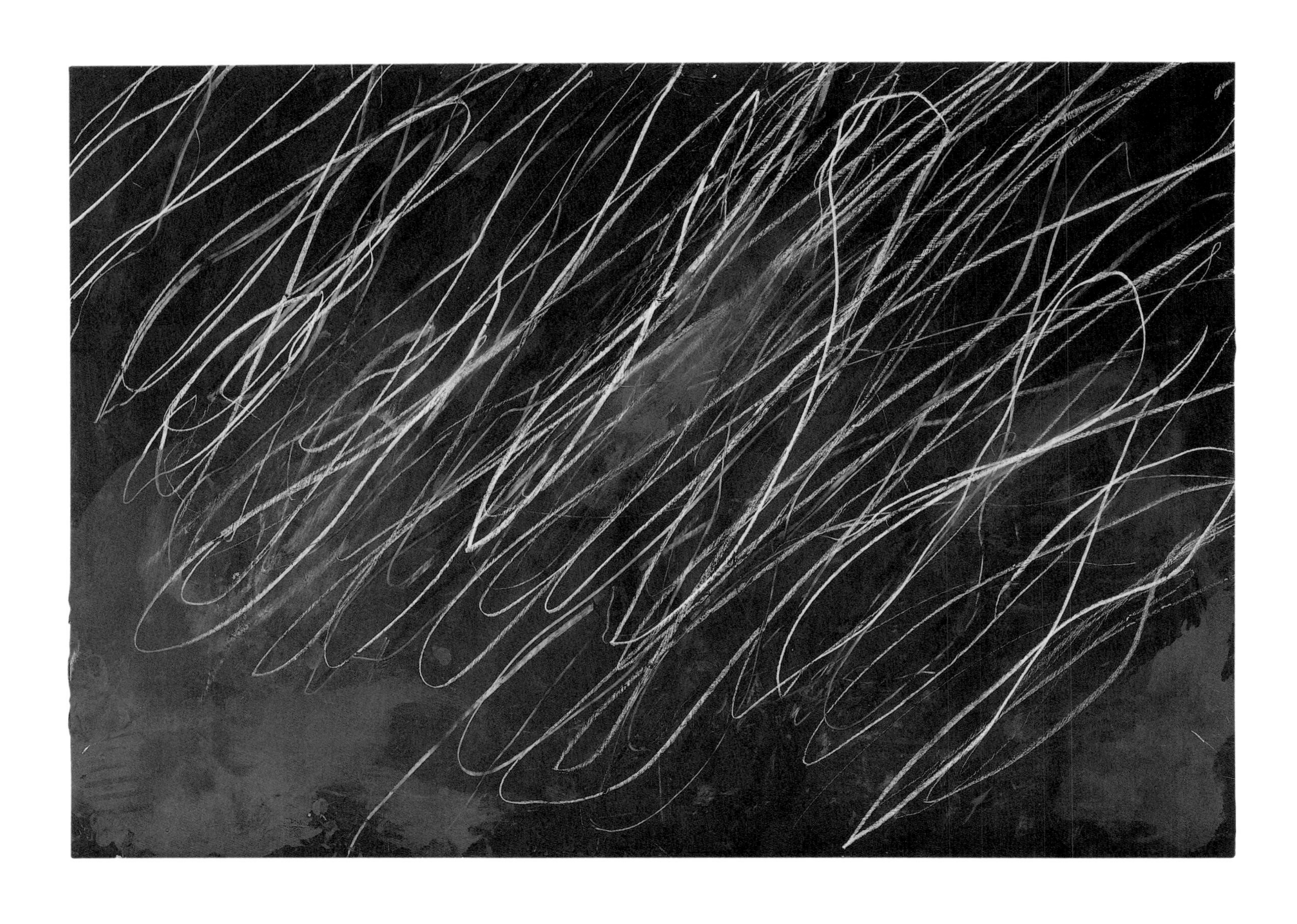

22. Untitled, 1970
Wax crayon, house paint
27 ¾ x 39 ⅜ in. (70.5 x 100 cm)

23. Untitled, 1969
Wax crayon, house paint
27 9/16 x 34 1/4 in. (70 x 87 cm)

24. Untitled, 1970
Wax crayon, house paint
27 3/4 x 39 3/8 in. (70.5 x 100 cm)

25. Untitled, 1970
Pencil, plywood, color pencil, oil paint, wax crayon, scotch tape
20 1/16 x 28 1/2 in. (51 x 72.3 cm)

26. Untitled, 1970
Pencil, plywood, color pencil, wax crayon, scotch tape, ink stamp
27 ⁹⁄₁₆ x 39 ⁹⁄₁₆ in. (70 x 100.5 cm)

27. Study for Treatise of the Veil, 1970
Wax crayon, pencil, color pencil, collage, scotch tape
27 ¾ x 39 ⅜ in. (70.5 x 100 cm)

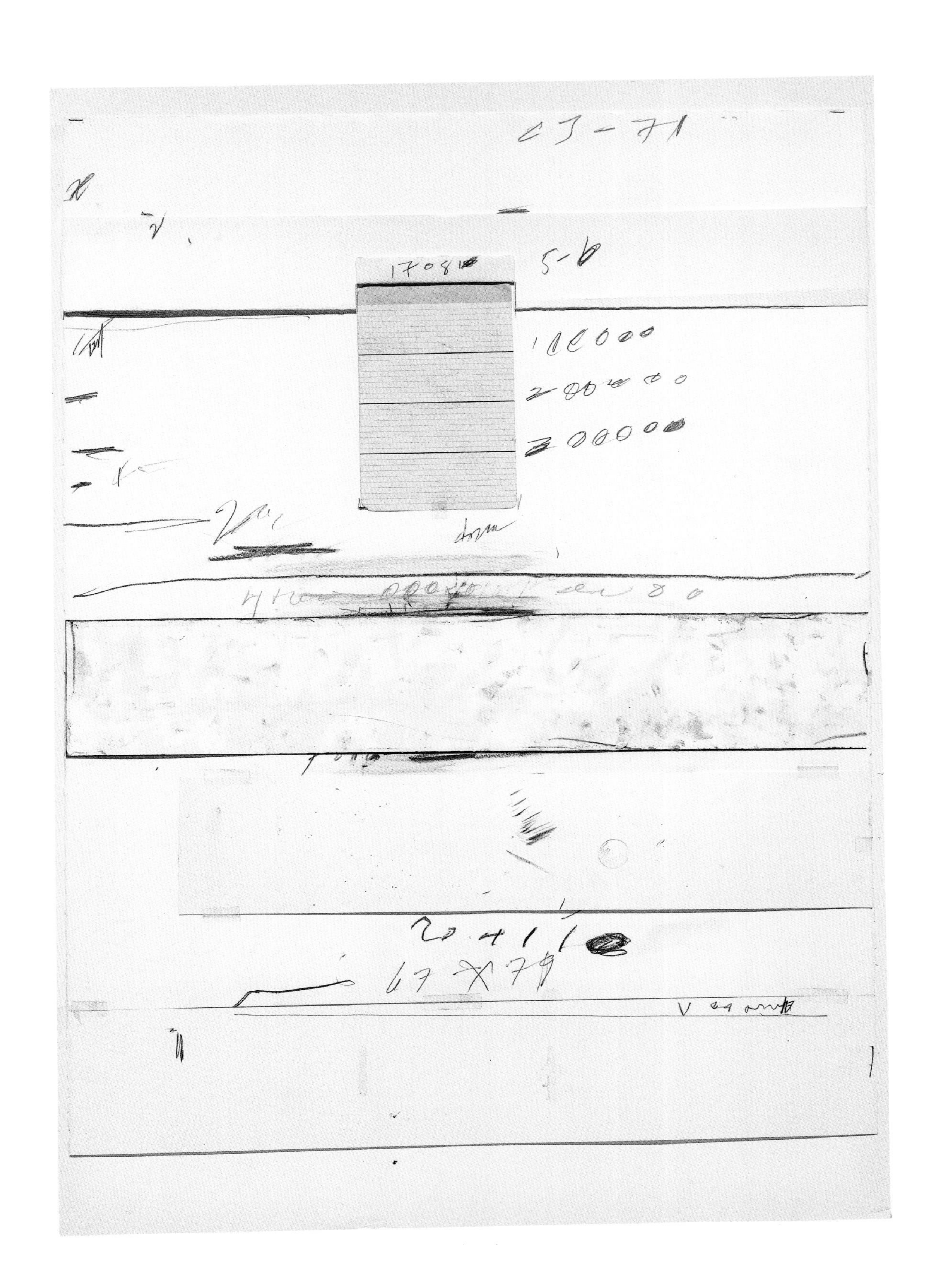

28. Untitled, 1971
Pencil, color pencil, wax crayon, collage
39 3/8 x 27 15/16 in. (100 x 71 cm)

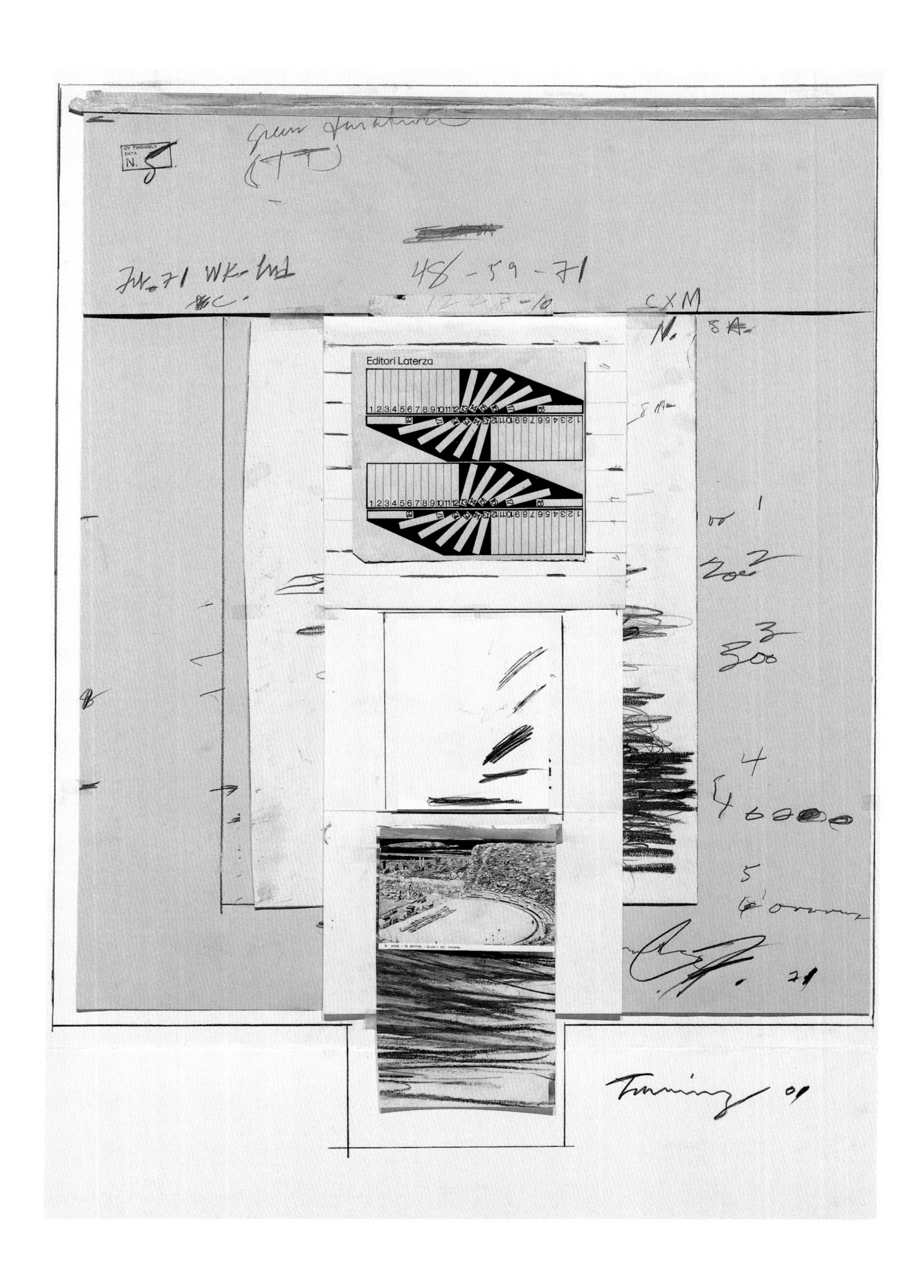

29. Untitled, 1971

Pencil, wax crayon, scotch tape, ink stamp, collage

39 3/8 x 27 9/16 in. (100 x 70 cm)

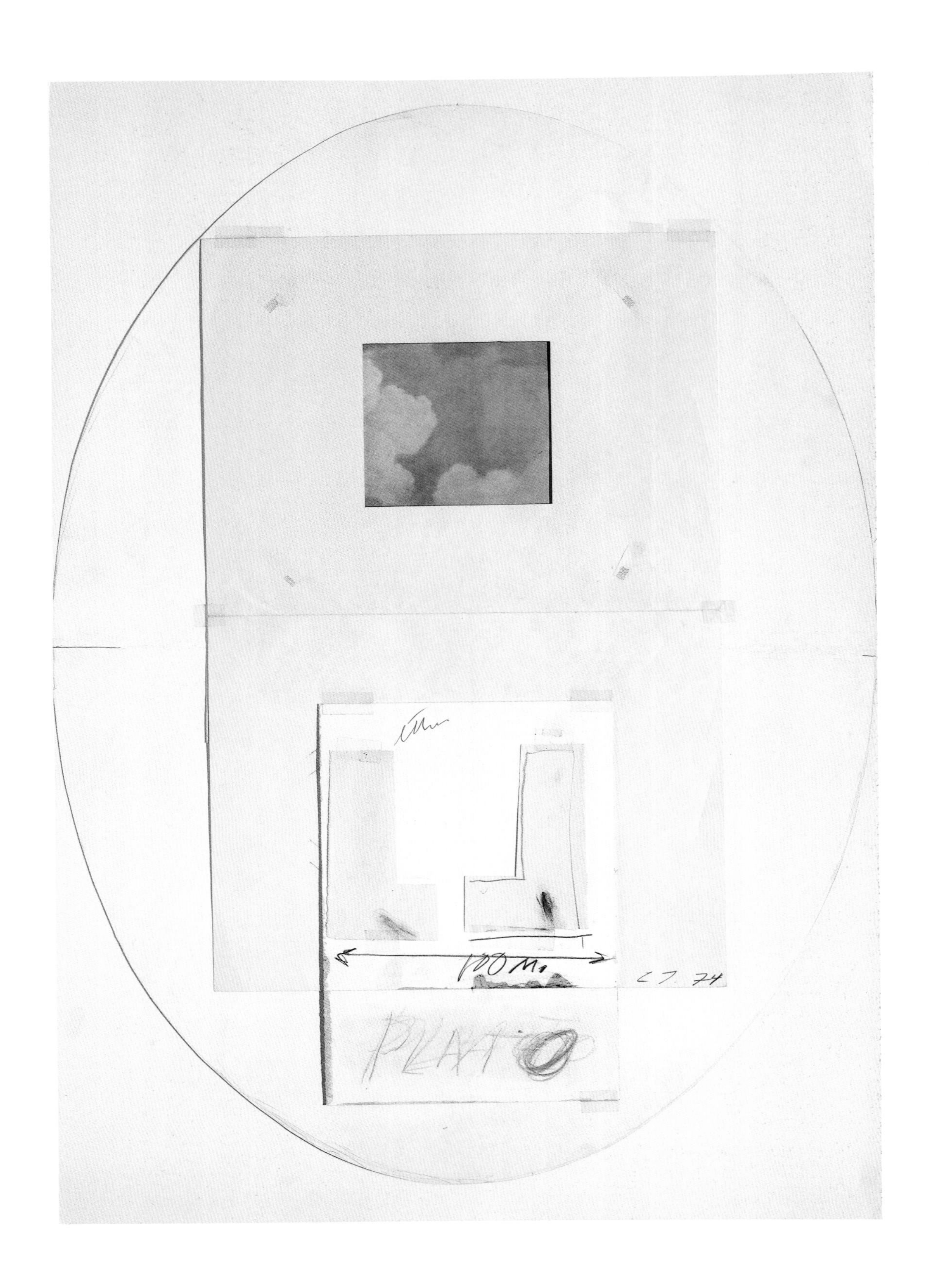

30. Plato, 1974
Pencil, color pencil, wax crayon, scotch tape, collage
39 1/8 x 27 9/16 in. (100 x 70 cm)

31. UNTITLED, 1974
Wax crayon, pencil, scotch tape, collage
29 1/2 x 41 1/4 in. (75 x 106 cm)

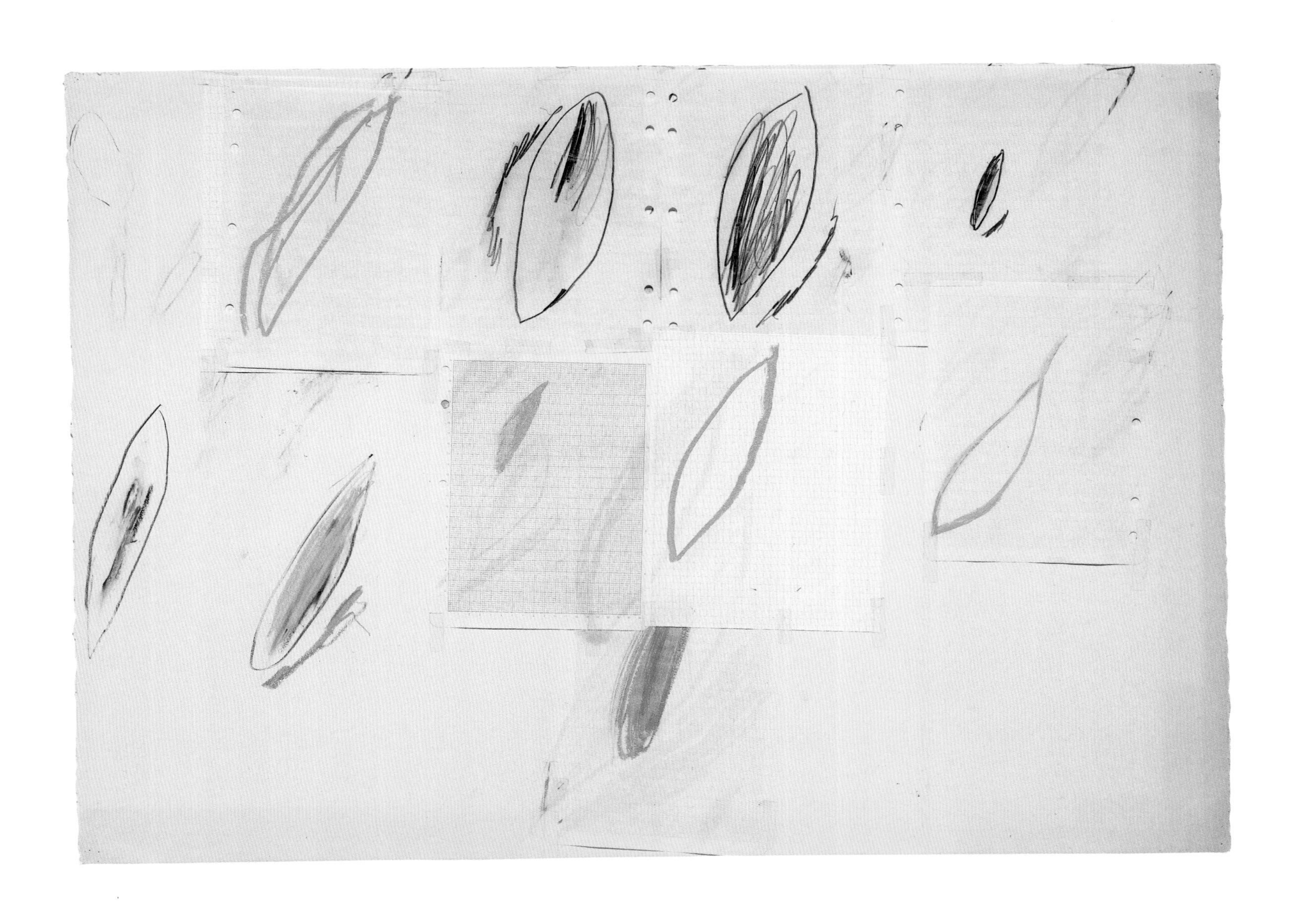

32. Untitled, 1975
Wax crayon, pencil, scotch tape, collage
29 1/2 x 41 3/4 in. (75 x 106 cm)

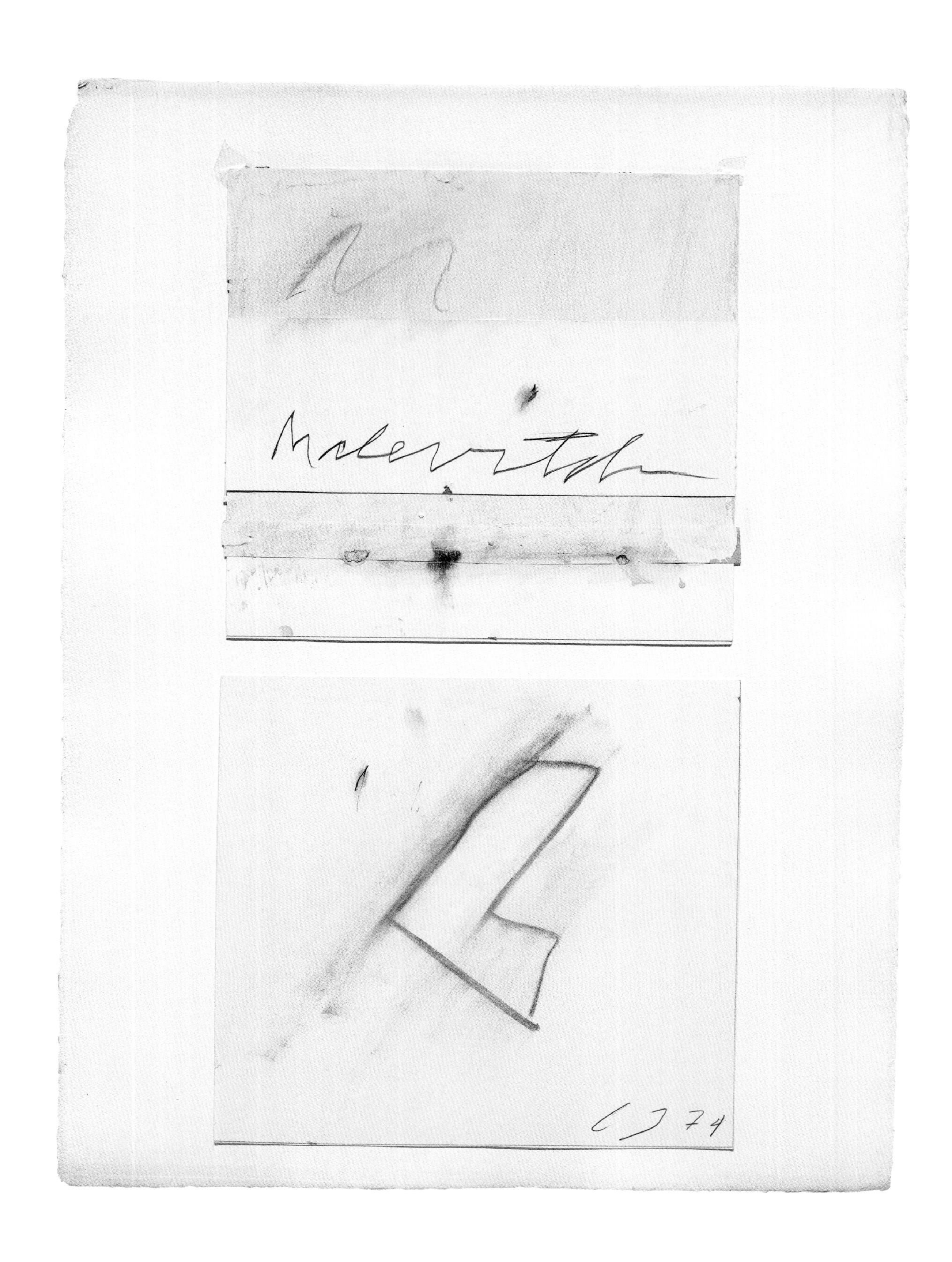

33. MALEVITCH, 1974
Pencil, oil paint, scotch tape, collage
30 7/8 x 22 13/16 in. (78.5 x 58 cm)

34. Tatlin, 1974
Pencil, wax crayon, oil paint, scotch tape, collage
30 5/16 x 22 in. (77 x 56 cm)

35. Orpheus, 1975
Oil paint, pencil, color pencil, scotch tape, collage
55 1/8 x 39 3/8 in. (140 x 100 cm)

36. Adonais, 1975
Oil paint, wax crayon, pencil, collage
65 3/8 x 46 7/8 in. (166 x 119 cm)

37. Apollo and the Artist, 1975
Oil paint, wax crayon, collage, pencil
55 7/8 x 50 3/8 in. (142 x 128 cm)

38. Mars and the Artist, 1975
Oil paint, wax crayon, pencil, collage
55 7/8 x 50 3/8 in. (142 x 128 cm)

39. Pan, 1975
Wax crayon, collage
58 1/4 x 39 3/8 in. (148 x 100 cm)

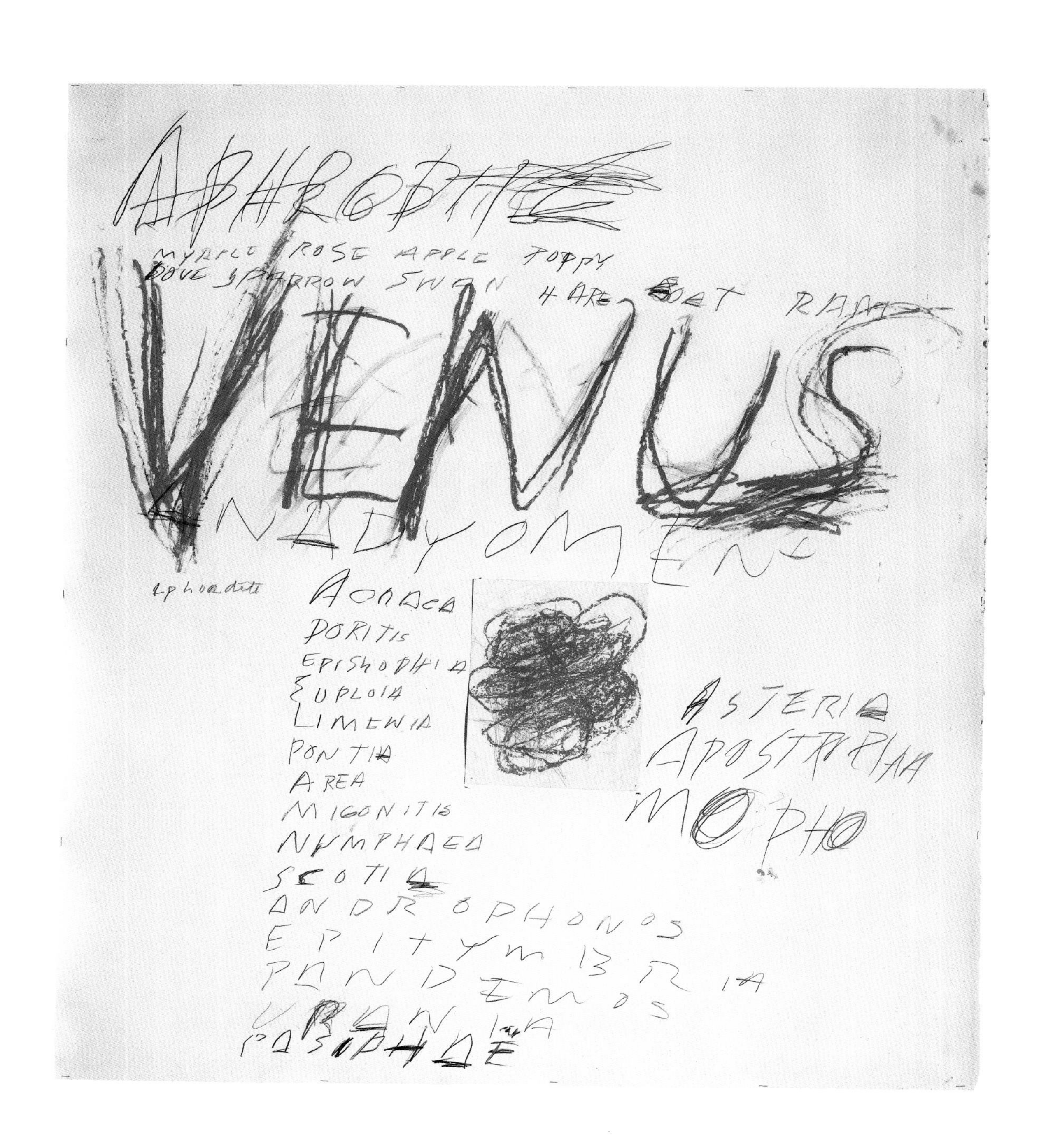

40. Venus, 1975
Oil stick, pencil, collage
59 1/16 x 53 15/16 in. (150 x 137 cm)

41. Apollo, 1975
Oil stick, pencil
59 9/16 x 53 1/4 in. (150 x 134 cm)

42. Bassano in Teverina, 1976
Pencil, color pencil, collage, glue
$32\frac{1}{2}$ x $22\frac{7}{16}$ in. (82.5 x 57 cm)

43. UNTITLED, 1981
Oil stick, oil paint, pencil
34 7/8 x 27 3/4 in. (88.5 x 70.5 cm)

44. NIMPHIDIA, 1981
Oil stick, oil paint, pencil
39 3/8 x 27 3/4 in. (100 x 70.5 cm)

45. Nimphidia, 1981
Oil stick, oil paint, pencil
39 ³⁄₈ x 27 ³⁄₄ in. (100 x 70.5 cm)

46. UNTITLED, 1982
Oil stick, oil paint, pencil, color pencil
39 3/8 x 27 9/16 in. (100 x 70 cm)

47. HRIH, 1982
Oil stick, pencil, color pencil
39 3/8 x 27 9/16 in. (100 x 70 cm)

48. Untitled, 1982
Oil stick, pencil, color pencil
39 3/8 x 27 9/16 in. (100 x 70 cm)

49. Anabasis, 1983
Oil stick, oil paint, pencil
39 3/8 x 27 9/16 in. (100 x 70 cm)

50. Victory, 1984
Oil stick, oil paint, pencil, collage
66 1/8 x 46 7/8 in. (168 x 119 cm)

51. PROTEUS, 1984
Acrylic paint, color pencil, pencil
$29\frac{15}{16}$ x $22\frac{1}{4}$ in. (76 x 56.5 cm)

52. PROTEUS, 1984
Acrylic paint, color pencil, pencil
29 15/16 x 22 1/4 in. (76 x 56.5 cm)

53./54. SCENES FROM AN IDEAL MARRIAGE, 1986
Acrylic paint, pencil
21¼ x 28¾ in. (54 x 73 cm)

55./56. SCENES FROM AN IDEAL MARRIAGE, 1986
Acrylic paint, pencil
21 1/4 x 28 3/4 in. (54 x 73 cm)

57. Untitled, 1987
Acrylic paint
$22\frac{1}{4} \times 29\frac{15}{16}$ in. (56.5 x 76 cm)

58. Untitled, 1987
Acrylic paint
22 1/4 x 29 15/16 in. (56.5 x 76 cm)

59. UNTITLED, 1987
Acrylic paint
22 1/4 x 29 15/16 in. (56.5 x 76 cm)

60. Untitled, 1987
Acrylic paint
$22\frac{1}{4}$ x $29\frac{15}{16}$ in. (56.5 x 76 cm)

61. UNTITLED, 1987
Acrylic paint, oil stick, pencil, collage
$39\frac{3}{16}$ x $27\frac{9}{16}$ in. (99.5 x 70 cm)

62. UNTITLED, 1989
Acrylic paint, color pencil, collage
40 15/16 x 29 1/2 in. (104 x 75 cm)

63. PETALS OF FIRE, 1989
Acrylic paint, oil stick, pencil, color pencil
56 $^{11}/_{16}$ x 50 $^{3}/_{8}$ in. (144 x 128 cm)

64. Petals of Fire, 1989
Acrylic paint, oil stick, pencil, color pencil
56 11/16 x 50 3/8 in. (144 x 128 cm)

65. Liri, 1990
Acrylic paint, oil stick, pencil, color pencil
30 11/16 x 22 in. (78 x 56 cm)

66. Untitled, 1990
Acrylic paint, oil stick, pencil, color pencil
30 1/16 x 22 in. (76.5 x 56 cm)

67. UNTITLED, 1990
Acrylic paint, oil stick, pencil, color pencil
27 ¾ x 22 in. (70.5 x 56 cm)

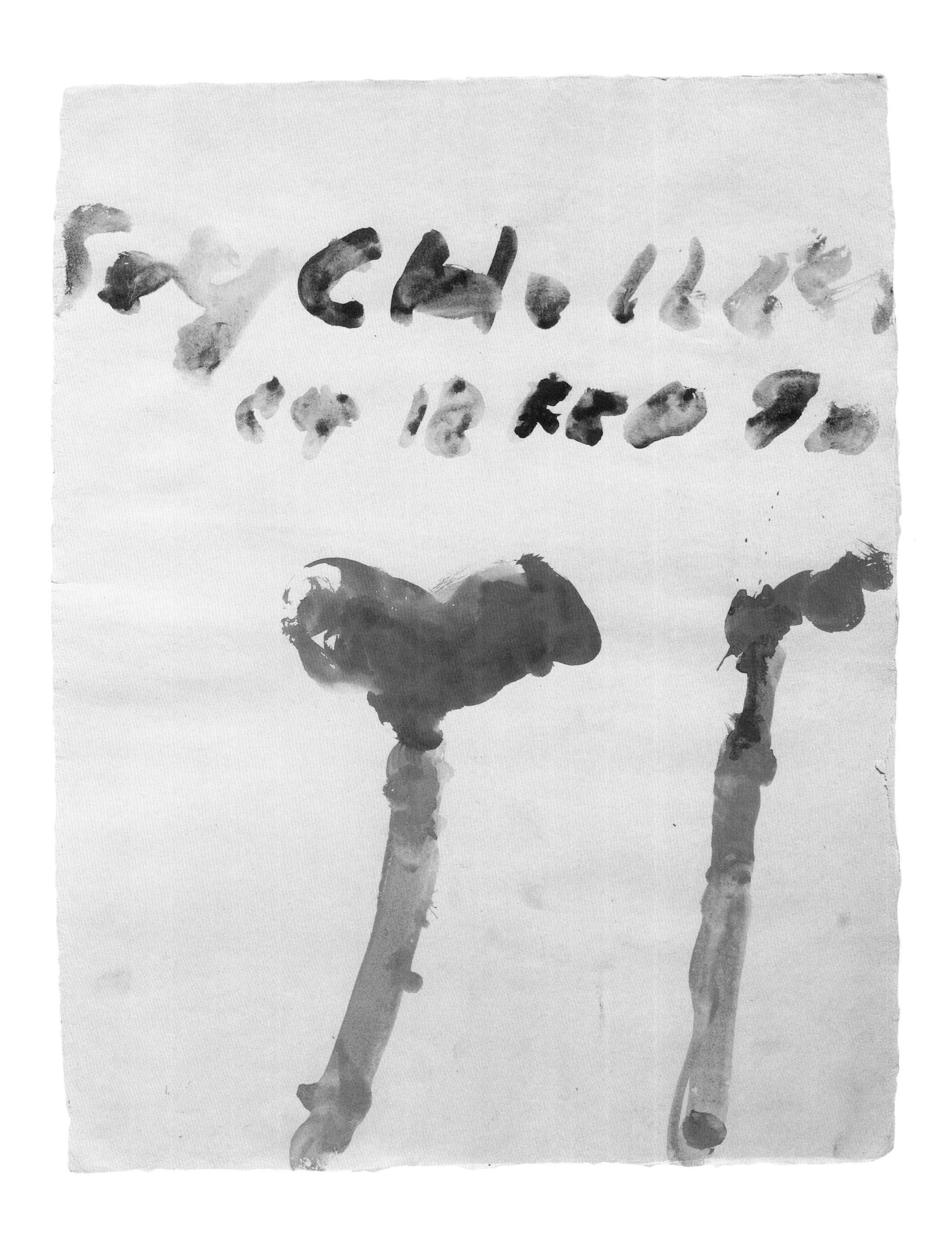

68. Seychelles, 1990
Acrylic paint
30 1/16 x 22 in. (76.5 x 56.5 cm)

69. Souvenir d'Arros, 1990
Acrylic paint
30 1/16 x 22 7/16 in. (76.5 x 57 cm)

70. Nicola's Irises, 1990
Acrylic paint
30½ x 22 in. (77.5 x 56 cm)

71. Untitled, 1990
Acrylic paint
29 15/16 x 22 7/16 in. (76 x 57 cm)

72. Untitled, 1991
Acrylic paint
30 1/16 x 22 in. (76.5 x 56 cm)

73. Untitled, 1990
Acrylic paint, ink, color pencil, collage
41 5/16 x 29 15/16 in. (105 x 71 cm)

74. Naumachia, 1992
Acrylic paint, pencil
29 15/16 x 22 in. (76 x 56 cm)
Collection of Larry Gagosian

75. Untitled, 2001
Acrylic paint, wax crayon, pencil, collage
48 13/16 x 39 in. (124 x 99 cm)

76. Untitled, 2001
Acrylic paint, wax crayon, pencil, collage
48 14/16 x 39 in. (124 x 99 cm)
The Judith Rothschild Foundation Contemporary Drawings Collection

77. Untitled, 2001
Acrylic paint, wax crayon, pencil, collage
48 $^{11}/_{16}$ x 39 in. (124 x 99 cm)

78. Untitled, 2001
Acrylic paint, wax crayon, pencil, collage
48 $^{13}/_{16}$ x 35 in. (124 x 89 cm)

79. UNTITLED, 2001
Acrylic paint, wax crayon
48 13/16 x 37 3/8 in. (124 x 95 cm)

80. Untitled, 2002
Monotype in acrylic paint on newspaper
23 5/8 x 17 11/16 in. (60 x 45 cm)

81. Untitled, 2002
Monotype in acrylic paint on newspaper
23 5/8 x 17 11/16 in. (60 x 45 cm)

82. Untitled, 1984–2002
Handmade book, crayon, watercolor, acrylic
15 ¾ x 22 ¹³⁄₁₆ in. (40 x 58 cm)

83. Untitled, 1984–2002
Handmade book, crayon, watercolor, acrylic
15 3/4 x 22 13/16 in. (40 x 58 cm)

84. UNTITLED, 1984–2002
Handmade book, crayon, watercolor, acrylic
15 3/4 x 22 13/16 in. (40 x 58 cm)

LIST OF PLATES

1. Untitled, 1953
Monotype in paint
18 7/8 x 25 3/16 in. (48 x 64 cm)

2. Untitled, 1953
Monotype in paint
18 7/8 x 25 3/16 in. (48 x 64 cm)

3. Untitled, 1953
Pencil
25 3/16 x 34 1/4 in. (64 x 87 cm)

4. Untitled, 1953
Pencil
25 3/16 x 34 1/4 in. (64 x 87 cm)

5. Untitled, 1954
Color pencil
19 1/16 x 25 3/16 in. (48.5 x 64 cm)

6. Untitled, 1954
Color pencil, crayon
19 1/16 x 25 3/16 in. (48.5 x 64 cm)

7. Untitled, 1954
Color pencil, crayon
19 1/16 x 25 3/16 in. (48.5 x 64 cm)

8. Untitled, 1954
Pencil, house paint
43 1/4 x 54 1/4 in. (110 x 138 cm)

9. Untitled, 1956
Pencil
22 x 30 1/8 in. (56 x 76.5 cm)

10. Untitled, 1956
Pencil
22 x 30 1/8 in. (56 x 76.5 cm)

11. Untitled, 1957
House paint, pencil, color paint
27 3/16 x 38 11/16 in. (69 x 98.3 cm)

12. Untitled, 1957
House paint, pencil, color paint
27 9/16 x 38 3/8 in. (70 x 100 cm)

13. Untitled, 1959
Collage, glue
33 1/2 x 24 3/8 in. (85 x 62 cm)

14. Untitled, 1961/63
Pencil, color pencil, ballpoint pen
19 11/16 x 28 in. (50 x 71 cm)

15. Untitled, 1961
Pencil, color pencil, ballpoint pen
19 11/16 x 27 15/16 in. (50 x 71 cm)

16. Bolsena, 1969
Pencil, color pencil, felt pen
57 1/4 x 71 1/16 in. (145.5 x 180.5 cm)

17. Bolsena, 1969
Pencil, color pencil, felt pen
57 1/4 x 71 1/16 in. (145.5 x 180.5 cm)

18. Bolsena, 1969
Pencil, color pencil
27 9/16 x 39 3/8 in. (70 x 100 cm)

19. Bolsena, 1969
Pencil, color pencil
27 9/16 x 39 3/8 in. (70 x 100 cm)

20. Untitled, 1971
Wax crayon, house paint
27 3/4 x 39 3/8 in. (70.5 x 100 cm)

21. Untitled, 1970
Wax crayon, house paint
27 9/16 x 34 1/4 in. (70 x 87 cm)

22. Untitled, 1970
Wax crayon, house paint
27 3/4 x 39 3/8 in. (70.5 x 100 cm)

23. Untitled, 1969
Wax crayon, house paint
27 9/16 x 34 1/4 in. (70 x 87 cm)

24. Untitled, 1970
Wax crayon, house paint
27 3/4 x 39 3/8 in. (70.5 x 100 cm)

25. Untitled, 1970
Pencil, plywood, color pencil, oil paint, wax crayon, scotch tape
20 1/16 x 28 1/2 in. (51 x 72.3 cm)

26. Untitled, 1970
Pencil, plywood, color pencil, wax crayon, scotch tape, ink stamp
27 9/16 x 39 9/16 in. (70 x 100.5 cm)

27. Study for Treatise of the Veil, 1970
Wax crayon, pencil, color pencil, collage, scotch tape
27 3/4 x 39 3/8 in. (70.5 x 100 cm)

28. Untitled, 1971
Pencil, color pencil, wax crayon, collage
39 3/8 x 27 15/16 in. (100 x 71 cm)

29. Untitled, 1971
Pencil, wax crayon, scotch tape, ink stamp, collage
39 3/8 x 27 9/16 in. (100 x 70 cm)

30. Plato, 1974
Pencil, color pencil, wax crayon, scotch tape, collage
39 3/8 x 27 9/16 in. (100 x 70 cm)

31. Untitled, 1974
Wax crayon, pencil, scotch tape, collage
29 1/2 x 41 3/4 in. (75 x 106 cm)

32. Untitled, 1975
Wax crayon, pencil, scotch tape, collage
29 1/2 x 41 3/4 in. (75 x 106 cm)

33. Malevitch, 1974
Pencil, oil paint, scotch tape, collage
30 7/8 x 22 13/16 in. (78.5 x 58 cm)

34. Tatlin, 1974
Pencil, wax crayon, oil paint, scotch tape, collage
30 5/16 x 22 in. (77 x 56 cm)

35. Orpheus, 1975
Oil paint, pencil, color pencil, scotch tape, collage
55 1/8 x 39 3/8 in. (140 x 100 cm)

36. Adonais, 1975
Oil paint, wax crayon, pencil, collage
65 3/8 x 46 7/8 in. (166 x 119 cm)

37. Apollo and the Artist, 1975
Oil paint, wax crayon, collage, pencil
55 7/8 x 50 3/8 in. (142 x 128 cm)

38. Mars and the Artist, 1975
Oil paint, wax crayon, pencil, collage
55 7/8 x 50 3/8 in. (142 x 128 cm)

39. Pan, 1975
Wax crayon, collage
58 1/4 x 39 3/8 in. (148 x 100 cm)

40. Venus, 1975
Oil stick, pencil, collage
59 1/16 x 53 15/16 in. (150 x 137 cm)

41. Apollo, 1975
Oil stick, pencil
59 1/16 x 53 3/4 in. (150 x 134 cm)

42. Bassano in Teverina, 1976
Pencil, color pencil, collage, glue
32 1/2 x 22 7/16 in. (82.5 x 57 cm)

43. Untitled, 1981
Oil stick, oil paint, pencil
34 7/8 x 27 3/4 in. (88.5 x 70.5 cm)

44. Nimphidia, 1981
Oil stick, oil paint, pencil
39 3/8 x 27 3/4 in. (100 x 70.5 cm)

45. Nimphidia, 1981
Oil stick, oil paint, pencil
39 3/8 x 27 3/4 in. (100 x 70.5 cm)

46. Untitled, 1982
Oil stick, oil paint, pencil, color pencil
39 3/8 x 27 9/16 in. (100 x 70 cm)

47. HRIH, 1982
Oil stick, pencil, color pencil
39 3/8 x 27 9/16 in. (100 x 70 cm)

48. Untitled, 1982
Oil stick, pencil, color pencil
39 3/8 x 27 9/16 in. (100 x 70 cm)

49. Anabasis, 1983
Oil stick, oil paint, pencil
39 3/8 x 27 9/16 in. (100 x 70 cm)

50. Victory, 1984
Oil stick, oil paint, pencil, collage
66 1/8 x 46 7/8 in. (168 x 119 cm)

51. Proteus, 1984
Acrylic paint, color pencil, pencil
29 15/16 x 22 1/4 in. (76 x 56.5 cm)

52. Proteus, 1984
Acrylic paint, color pencil, pencil
29 15/16 x 22 1/4 in. (76 x 56.5 cm)

53. Scenes from an Ideal Marriage, 1986
Acrylic paint, pencil
21 1/4 x 28 3/4 in. (54 x 73 cm)

54. Scenes from an Ideal Marriage, 1986
Acrylic paint, pencil
21 1/4 x 28 3/4 in. (54 x 73 cm)

55. Scenes from an Ideal Marriage, 1986
Acrylic paint, pencil
21 1/4 x 28 3/4 in. (54 x 73 cm)

56. Scenes from an Ideal Marriage, 1986
Acrylic paint, pencil
21 1/4 x 28 3/4 in. (54 x 73 cm)

57. Untitled, 1987
Acrylic paint
22 1/4 x 29 15/16 in. (56.5 x 76 cm)

58. Untitled, 1987
Acrylic paint
22 1/4 x 29 15/16 in. (56.5 x 76 cm)

59. Untitled, 1987
Acrylic paint
22 1/4 x 29 15/16 in. (56.5 x 76 cm)

60. Untitled, 1987
Acrylic paint
22 1/4 x 29 15/16 in. (56.5 x 76 cm)

61. Untitled, 1987
Acrylic paint, oil stick, pencil, collage
39 3/16 x 27 9/16 in. (99.5 x 70 cm)

62. Untitled, 1989
Acrylic paint, color pencil, collage
40 15/16 x 29 1/2 in. (104 x 75 cm)

63. Petals of Fire, 1989
Acrylic paint, oil stick, pencil, color pencil
56 11/16 x 50 3/8 in. (144 x 128 cm)

64. Petals of Fire, 1989
Acrylic paint, oil stick, pencil, color pencil
56 11/16 x 50 3/8 in. (144 x 128 cm)

65. Liri, 1990
Acrylic paint, oil stick, pencil, color pencil
30 11/16 x 22 in. (78 x 56 cm)

66. Untitled, 1990
Acrylic paint, oil stick, pencil, color pencil
30 1/16 x 22 in. (76.5 x 56 cm)

67. Untitled, 1990
Acrylic paint, oil stick, pencil, color pencil
27 3/4 x 22 in. (70.5 x 56 cm)

68. Seychelles, 1990
Acrylic paint
30 1/16 x 22 in. (76.5 x 56.5 cm)

69. Souvenir d'Arros, 1990
Acrylic paint
30 1/16 x 22 7/16 in. (76.5 x 57 cm)

70. Nicola's Irises, 1990
Acrylic paint
30 1/2 x 22 in. (77.5 x 56 cm)

71. Untitled, 1990
Acrylic paint
29 15/16 x 22 7/16 in. (76 x 57 cm)

72. Untitled, 1991
Acrylic paint
30 1/16 x 22 in. (76.5 x 56 cm)

73. Untitled, 1990
Acrylic paint, ink, color pencil, collage
41 5/16 x 29 15/16 in. (105 x 71 cm)

74. Naumachia, 1992
Acrylic paint, pencil
29 15/16 x 22 in. (76 x 56 cm)
Collection of Larry Gagosian

75. Untitled, 2001
Acrylic paint, wax crayon, pencil, collage
48 13/16 x 39 in. (124 x 99 cm)

76. Untitled, 2001
Acrylic paint, wax crayon, pencil, collage
48 14/16 x 39 in. (124 x 99 cm)
The Judith Rothschild Foundation
Contemporary Drawings Collection

77. Untitled, 2001
Acrylic paint, wax crayon, pencil, collage
48 13/16 x 39 in. (124 x 99 cm)

78. Untitled, 2001
Acrylic paint, wax crayon, pencil, collage
48 13/16 x 35 in. (124 x 89 cm)

79. Untitled, 2001
Acrylic paint, wax crayon
48 13/16 x 37 3/8 in. (124 x 95 cm)

80. Untitled, 2002
Monotype in acrylic paint on newspaper
23 5/8 x 17 11/16 in. (60 x 45 cm)

81. Untitled, 2002
Monotype in acrylic paint on newspaper
23 5/8 x 17 11/16 in. (60 x 45 cm)

82–84. Untitled, 1984–2002
Handmade books, crayon, watercolor, acrylic paint
15 3/4 x 22 13/16 in. (40 x 58 cm)

All works are on paper. Dimensions: height precedes width.
Unless otherwise noted, all works are in the collection of the artist.

BIOGRAPHICAL NOTES

1928 Cy Twombly was born in Lexington, Virginia, on April 25.

1942 From the age of 14 to 18, Twombly attended lectures on painting given by the artist Pierre Daura. Daura was a Spanish artist, a refugee in Paris during the civil war, who had married a woman from Virginia and come to live in Lexington. His lectures and studio classes focused on European contemporary art and its history.

1946 After graduating from Lexington High School, attended Darlington School for Boys in Rome, Georgia.

1947 Spent the summer in Ogunquit, an art colony in Maine, and in Groveland, Massachusetts. In the fall he enrolled at the Boston Museum School, where the teachers were primarily influenced by German Expressionism. Twombly was greatly interested in the Dada movement and the art of Kurt Schwitters and Chaim Soutine. He was also impressed by the works of Alberto Giacometti and Jean Dubuffet.

1948 Studied in Boston.

1949 Entered the newly established department of art of Washington and Lee University in Lexington.

1950 On a tuition scholarship, he continued his studies at the Art Students League in New York. His teachers were Will Barnett, Morris Kantor, and Vaclav Vytlacil. During the second semester he met another young artist, Robert Rauschenberg, with whom he shared the same intellectual interests. In New York he was able to see avant-garde shows such as Jackson Pollock, Mark Rothko, Barnett Newman, Clyfford Still, Robert Motherwell, and others at galleries such as Betty Parsons and Kootz Gallery, as well as the work of Willem de Kooning and Franz Kline at Egan Gallery.

1951 Attended the summer and winter semesters at Black Mountain College, North Carolina. Ben Shahn and Robert Motherwell were artists in residence that summer. In the month of November Twombly had his first one-artist exhibition at the Seven Stairs Gallery in Chicago, showing paintings completed that summer at Black Mountain College; the photographer Aaron Siskind and the curator Noah Goldowsky arranged the show. At the end of the year, Robert Motherwell sponsored Twombly's first exhibition in New York at the Kootz Gallery (a two-artist exhibition with Brody Gandy).

1952 Took trips to the South as far as Key West, Florida, and from there to Cuba. Worked in Virginia during the summer, visiting Black Mountain College, where Franz Kline, Robert Rauschenberg, Jack Tworkov, and John Cage were staying. In the fall Twombly received a traveling scholarship from the Virginia Museum of Fine Arts and left by boat for his first visit to Europe and North Africa. He disembarked in Palermo and went from Rome to Morocco, staying there for the winter, traveling to Casablanca, Marrakesh, the Atlas Mountains, and Tangier. He visited Paul Bowles in Tétouan and took day trips with him to surrounding villages. Returned to Rome by train, visiting Spain on his way back.

1953 In February Twombly had his first show in Italy at the Galleria di Via della Croce, 71. On March 14 in Florence at the Galleria d'arte contemporanea, he showed tapestries done in Tangier and Tétouan. In the late spring he returned to America to work on paintings, sculptures, and monoprints, using Robert Rauschenberg's New York studio on Fulton Street. In the fall he had a show at the Stable Gallery and in Princeton of drawings, paintings, and sculpture. Drafted into the army, he completed his basic training in Augusta, Georgia, and was stationed in Washington, DC, assigned to the department of coding and decoding. During weekends in Augusta he had rented a room in a hotel to produce drawings that would form the basis for his second one-artist show at the Stable Gallery.

1954 In August Twombly was discharged from the army. He stayed in New York, and started to work on *Panorama*. He also did plaster sculptures in the sand at Staten Island.

1955 In February he accepted a position in the art department of Southern Seminary in Buena Vista, Virginia, for one year. A show at Catholic University, Washington, DC, of Twombly's early works in conjunction with African sculptures was arranged by a priest whose field of interest was African sculptures. In the fall he rented an apartment in New York on William Street, where he painted *The Geeks, Free Wheeler, Academy*, and other works, and made sculptures.

1956 Exhibited at the Stable Gallery in January.

1957 Twombly had his third one-artist show at the Stable Gallery in January, where *Panorama* was shown. He left New York to spend the summer in Italy; at the suggestion of the Italian painter Toti Scialoja, he took a house for the summer on the island of Procida in the Bay of Naples. Later in the fall he worked in an apartment in Rome, facing the Colloseum, where *Olympia, Arcadia, Blue Room*, and *Sunset* were painted. He also worked on drawings in Grottaferrata, in a friend's house near Rome, and later in a studio in Via Margutta (loaned by the artist Scarpitta).

1958 Worked in an empty house on Via Appia Pignatelli. He had his first exhibition in Rome at the Galleria La Tartaruga of Plinio De Martis, showing a selection of paintings.

1959 Returned to the United States in early spring and married Luisa (Tatiana) Franchetti in New York. He worked in a studio in Lexington on ten large paintings for an exhibition at Leo Castelli Gallery in New York, but the works were never shown. After a second trip to Cuba just after the revolution, he visited the Yucatán, Mexico, then returned to Rome. He rented an apartment for the summer in Sperlonga, a small whitewashed fishing village on the Tyrrhenian Sea. In December his son, Cyrus Alessandro, was born in Rome. Twombly lived in Rome in Via Belsiana, where he did some sculptures and painted *Age of Alexander* on New Year's Eve.

1960 Twombly moved to Via Monserrato, where he painted *To Leonardo, Crimes of Passion, Odeion, Sunset Series, School of Fontainbleau, Sahara*, and *Herodiade*. He had a second exhibition in April at the Galleria La Tartaruga. He worked on a group of drawings during July in Sant' Angelo on the island of Ischia, traveling in August to Greece and in September to Castel Gardena in the Italian Dolomites. In October he had his first exhibition at Leo Castelli Gallery in New York.

1961 Worked for the next five years in a studio he rented in Piazza del Biscione. That year, among other works, he painted *Triumph of Galatea*, *Empire of Flora*, and *Bay of Naples*. He worked on the series of the five *Ferragosto* paintings in his Via Monserrato house, where he also painted *School of Athens* and *Bay of Naples*. June and July were spent on the Greek island of Mykonos, working on a large group of drawings titled *Delian Odes*. Some of these drawings were destroyed by neighborhood children who had come into the studio drawn by curiosity. He returned to Italy and spent September in Castel Gardena in the Dolomites. A selection of works from 1954 to 1960 was published in the first comprehensive catalogue of Twombly's work by the Galleria La Tartaruga.

1962 In January and February he took a sailing trip down the Nile as far south as Wadi Halfa in the Sudan. He spent the summer sailing in the Dodecanese islands in Greece and along the coast of Turkey. In the Piazza del Biscione studio he painted *Birth of Venus*, *Hero and Leander*, *Leda and the Swan*, *Hyperion (to Keats)*, *Dutch Interior*, and *Second Voyage to Italy*.

1963 Visited Sicily during January and February, staying in the town of Menfi. He spent the summer in Sperlonga, had shows in Cologne, Turin, and Geneva, and in December he painted in nine parts *Discourse on Commodus* in the Piazza del Biscione studio.

1964 In March Twombly exhibited at Leo Castelli Gallery in New York the nine-part painting called *Discourse on Commodus*, a cycle that refers to the different psychological stages in the life and death of the emperor Commodus. He spent the spring in Greece and in July and August worked in Castel Gardena on a series of drawings called *Notes from a Tower*. In the fall he went to Munich to prepare a show for the Galerie Friedrich + Dahlem. One of the owners of the gallery was Heiner Friedrich, who later had a great influence on the forming of the Dia Art Foundation. Twombly called the series of paintings he exhibited in Munich *The Artist in the Northern Climate*.

1965 The first large museum show of Twombly's works opened at the Museum Haus Lange of Krefeld, an exhibition shown subsequently in Brussels at the Palais des Beaux Arts and at the Stedelijk Museum in Amsterdam. He spent the summer traveling in Mykonos, Patmos, Samos, and along the Turkish coast. In the fall he worked in New York in a studio on 52nd Street, where he did a series of drawings.

1966 On returning to New York from a visit to Lexington, Twombly had a show at Leo Castelli Gallery featuring drawings he had done in New York. He traveled back to Rome in the spring and started to work on the gray paintings, whose iconography would be the theme for the work of the next several years. After spending the summer in Castel Gardena and Sant' Angelo in Ischia, he returned to New York in the fall, again working at the apartment on 52nd Street.

1967 In January Twombly used the loft of David Whitney at 11 Canal Street in New York while working on a second series of gray paintings. The Galleria Notizie in Turin showed the first group of gray paintings completed in Rome the year before. He went back to Italy to spend the summer. In October the Leo Castelli Gallery in New York showed, for the first time in the United States, the artist's new gray paintings, featuring the works created in the loft on Canal Street. He spent October and November working in New York and Lexington, as well as executing a series of etchings at Tania Grossmann on Long Island. He returned by boat to Italy at the end of November.

1968 In January the Milwaukee Art Center presented the first large museum show in the United States to provide a comprehensive selection of Twombly's works from 1956 onward. Twombly took a studio on 356 Bowery in New York, which he kept for a number of years. There he painted the series of three *Orion* pictures and *Synopsis of a Battle*, *Veil of Orpheus*, and *Treatise of the Veil*. He spent August in Castel Gardena, returning in the fall to New York to work in the Bowery studio. In November he spent a short time on Captiva Island, Florida, in Rauschenberg's house, working on a series of collages that used motifs from Leonardo da Vinci's studies of anatomy, weather, and drapery. Nicholas Wilder Gallery in Los Angeles showed the gray paintings from the Bowery studio in December. From Los Angeles Twombly traveled to Mexico, visiting different sites and staying in a small coastal village in the jungle along the Pacific called Yalapa.

1969 Returning from Mexico to New York, Twombly next traveled to the Caribbean island of St. Martin, staying part of January and February in the village of Grand Case. Here he made a series of drawings whose images he later developed into the paintings of the *Bolsena* series. The following summer he rented an apartment in Palazzo del Drago on Bolsena Lake, where he painted the large paintings of the *Bolsena* series.

1970 Worked in New York in the Bowery studio, visited Lexington, and spent the month of March on Captiva Island. He visited Ireland in the summer, returning to Rome, where he painted the second version of *Treatise of the Veil* in Via Monserrato. Gabriele Stocchi published for addenda editore *Cy Twombly. 11 Grey Paintings 1967–1970*, including etching.

1971 In February the Galleria Gian Enzo Sperone in Turin showed Twombly's new works. He also had a show in Paris at Yvon Lambert that included paintings and gouaches. He spent the summer in Anacapri at the Villa Orlando working on drawings and collages. At the beginning of the fall he worked in Rome on the group of five "Nini's" paintings, in response to the tragic death of Nini Pirandello, the wife of his first gallery patron in Rome, Plinio De Martis. Twombly went back to New York in November and spent the rest of the year on Captiva Island doing a series of lithographs for Untitled Press.

1972 In January the Leo Castelli Gallery showed three large untitled paintings. On his return to Rome in the spring, Twombly started to work on a very large canvas whose title was *Anatomy of Melancholy*, in reference to the book written by Robert Burton in the seventeenth century. Twombly finished this painting twenty-two years later in Lexington; he gave it the title *Say Goodbye Catullus to the Shores of Asia Minor*. He spent the summer in Capri and the winter on Captiva Island, working on drawings.

1973 A retrospective was organized in April at the Kunsthalle of Bern, then traveled to Munich at the Lenbachhaus. At the same time, the Kunstmuseum of Basel organized a large show of drawings. In the summer, in Castel Gardena, he completed the drawings titled *24 Short Pieces*. He traveled in the fall to India.

1974 Spent February on Captiva Island. He had gallery exhibitions in Munich, Turin, Paris, and Naples. He worked on a portfolio of prints titled *Natural History—Part I*.

1975 Spent the winter on Captiva Island. Took a fifteenth-century house in Bassano (in Teverina, north of Rome near Bomarzo) and worked at restoring it over the next three years, adding a studio where he would work in the summers for the following years. In March a representative group of paintings, drawings, and sculptures was shown at the Institute for Contemporary Art in Philadelphia. The exhibition traveled to the San Francisco Museum of Modern Art. On returning to Rome, he took a trip to Tunisia. At the end of May he was back in Rome, working on two large-scale collages titled *Mars and the Artist* and *Apollo and the Artist*.

1976 Worked during the winter in the attic of the Hotel Excelsior in Naples, preparing for a show at the Galleria Lucio Amelio, then went to Captiva Island at the end of February. He had an exhibition of drawings from 1954 to 1976 at the Musée d'art moderne de la ville de Paris, ARC 2. In September the Leo Castelli Gallery showed a group of watercolors that Twombly had painted in New York during the month of May. An exhibition opened in Rome at the Galleria Gian Enzo Sperone featuring large-scale works on paper like *Leda and the Swan*, *Idilli*, and *Narcissus*. Worked on prints, *Natural History—part II*, and *Some Trees of Italy*. He also started to work on sculptures again.

1977 That summer in his studio in Bassano, Twombly finished a large three-panel painting titled *Thyrsis*. Reading Alexander Pope's translation of the *Iliad* inspired him to work on *Fifty Days at Iliam*, a large ten-painting cycle.

1978 That summer in Bassano, he finished *Fifty Days at Iliam*, which was shown in November in New York at the Heiner Friedrich Lone Star Foundation. He painted that same summer *Goethe in Italy*. In the fall Heiner Bastian published the first monograph on Twombly's paintings for Propyläen Verlag.

1979 The Galleria Lucio Amelio of Naples organized the first show of Twombly's sculptures, consisting of a selection of eleven sculptures from his work of the previous years. The Whitney Museum of American Art in New York opened in April a retrospective of works created from 1954 to 1977. Roland Barthes wrote the introduction of the catalogue to the Whitney retrospective. Yvon Lambert published the first volume (VI) of the catalogue raisonné of Twombly's drawings with an essay by Barthes. In May Twombly went from New York to Paris, where he met Barthes. He worked in Bassano in June and July and traveled that fall to Russia and Afghanistan. He spent the months of December and January 1980 on the Caribbean island of Iles des Saintes working on watercolors.

1980 Participated in the Venice Biennale with a cycle of drawings from that spring in Rome titled *5 Days Wait at Jiayuguan*. Gabriele Stocchi published a monograph on this series. He worked on a series of sculptures in summer.

1981 Worked on drawings and sculptures in a studio that he rented in late spring in a town called Formia on the gulf of Gaeta. In Bassano that summer he prepared for the show at Sperone Westwater Fischer Gallery in New York, which consisted of a group of works on paper. These works were exhibited the following year. The first museum show of his sculptures, consisting of twenty-three works from 1958 to 1981, opened at the Museum Haus Lange of Krefeld. A catalogue was published with an essay by Marianne Stockebrand. In the fall there was an exhibition of works on paper from 1954 to 1976 that traveled from Newport Beach, Harbor Art Museum, to Madison, Elvehjem Museum of Art, to Richmond, Virginia Museum of Fine Arts, and to Toronto, Art Gallery of Ontario. He traveled to the Greek island of Samos in September, then in November in Rome he painted the three large *Bacchus* works.

1982 In February he went to Key West, where he worked on drawings. He also stayed in New York and Lexington, working on a series of gouaches called *Notes from Silver Wood*.

1983 Returned to Italy, working in March in Gaeta, a medieval port on the Tyrrhenian Sea between Rome and Naples. He traveled to Yemen with his son Alessandro in June and worked during August in Bassano on the *Anabasis* drawings.

1984 During the winter in Key West, he completed a set of drawings called *Proteus*. In May the Musée d'art contemporain of Bordeaux inaugurated an exhibition of Twombly's works on paper. In the summer months he worked in Bassano on the three-part painting *Hero and Leander*. In September the Kunsthalle Baden-Baden presented a large exhibition of paintings and drawings. At the same time Twombly received from the authorities of Baden-Württemberg the "Internationaler Preis für bildende Kunst der Landes Baden-Württemberg." In October a show of his sculptures opened in Rome at the Galleria Sperone.

1985 Spent the winter months in Egypt, mostly in Luxor, and the rest of the year in Gaeta, using the house of a friend to work on sculptures.

1986 Twombly spent the spring in Gaeta and the summer in Bassano, completing the second version of *Hero and Leander (to Christopher Marlowe)* and *Analysis of the Rose as Sentimental Despair*. He designed and supervised the painting of the curtain for the Opéra Bastille in Paris. In August he completed a series of four untitled paintings. He lived during the fall and winter in Gaeta, where he took a house, supervising its restoration and the creation of a garden of lemon trees, conceived as a collection of rooms.

1987 Harald Szeemann organized a large retrospective of Twombly's work, including paintings, sculptures, and drawings, at the Kunsthaus of Zurich. The exhibition traveled to Madrid's Palacio de Velàzquez/Palacio de Cristal, London's Whitechapel Art Gallery, Düsseldorf's Städtische Kunsthalle, and the Centre Georges Pompidou in Paris. Twombly worked in the summer in Bassano. An exhibition of works on paper traveled from Bonn, Städtisches Kunstmuseum, to Barcelona, Centre Cultural de la Fundació Caixa de Pensions. He was elected a member of the American Academy and Institute of Arts and Letters in New York, and the city of Siegen in Germany awarded him the "Rubens Preis." He spent the fall and winter in Gaeta.

1988 Twombly worked in the spring in Gaeta on two large paintings on paper called *Venere Sopra Gaeta*, which were shown in Naples at the Galleria Lucio Amelio; one of these now exists only as fragments. He worked on sculptures in Gaeta and in Rome on a cycle of nine "green paintings," later shown at the Venice Biennale together with his sculptures. He received from the French government the "Chevalier dans l'Ordre des Arts et des Lettres." He spent the fall in the United States and the winter in Gaeta.

1989 In February an exhibition of Twombly's early paintings and sculptures from 1951 to 1953 opened in New York at the Sperone Westwater Gallery. In September the Menil Collection in Houston inaugurated a large exhibition of paintings, drawings, and sculptures. The exhibition traveled to the Des Moines Art Center. The large ten-painting work *Fifty Days at Iliam* was acquired and installed in a special room at the Philadelphia

Museum of Art. Twombly spent the month of October in the Seychelles islands. In December the Gagosian Gallery in New York assembled a show featuring eight of the *Bolsena* paintings. Twombly traveled in December to Istanbul.

1990 Returned to the Seychelles islands to spend the months of January and February, first on the island of La Digue, then on d'Arros island. There he worked on a series of drawings. He spent the spring in Gaeta working on another set of drawings. These two series of drawings were shown in the summer with a selection of sculptures at Thomas Ammann Fine Art in Zurich and later published in a 1992 book titled *Souvenirs of d'Arros and Gaeta* edited by Thomas Ammann. Twombly traveled in March to Zurich, Paris, and Madrid. He received in April the Skowhegan medal for painting. In Gaeta he painted several works titled *Summer and Madness*, finishing them in August in Bassano. He spent December in Sorrento.

1991 In Gaeta he worked on sculptures such as *Thermopylae*, which was shown in Paris at the Galerie Pièce-Unique later that fall. During the summer, he retraced the poet Byron's itinerary in Greece as far as Epirus, going after to the island of Syros. He started to work in July in Bassano on the two sets of the *Quattro Stagioni*. Volume VII of the catalogue raisonné of drawings from 1977 to 1982 was published by Yvon Lambert with an essay by Philip Sellers. He worked on sculptures in Gaeta that fall. The Kunsthaus in Zurich dedicated a space in the museum for the permanent exhibition of ten of his sculptures.

1992 Spent the winter on Jupiter Island, Florida, where he worked on a series of sculptures. He returned for the summer to Gaeta to complete a three-panel painting using the motif of sea and boats, which would become a recurrent subject for his works. The first volume of the catalogue raisonné of Twombly's paintings, by Heiner Bastian, was published in the fall. In the following years other catalogues raisonnés covering the entire paintings production would be published with essays by Heiner Bastian.

1993 Spent the beginning of the winter on Jupiter Island. In the spring, nostalgic for his hometown, he took a house in Lexington, where he would spend the spring and fall of the next years. He worked during the summer in Gaeta finishing *Autunno* and *Inverno* of the first set of the *Quattro Stagioni*. He received an honorary doctoral degree from Washington and Lee University.

1994 Spent the winter in Lexington and the spring and summer in Gaeta, where he completed the first set of the *Quattro Stagioni* and some sculptures. On returning to Lexington in the fall, he rented an empty warehouse, where he finished the long painting started in Rome twenty-two years earlier, *Say Goodbye Catullus to the Shores of Asia Minor*. At the end of September a large retrospective of Twombly's paintings, drawings, and sculptures, organized by Kirk Varnedoe, opened in New York at the Museum of Modern Art. The show traveled to the Menil Collection in Houston, to Los Angeles, and to Berlin's Neue Nationalgalerie. In September the Gagosian Gallery in New York showed the three-panel painting *Say Goodbye Catullus to the Shores of Asia Minor* for the first time; this painting was shown the next year in Houston at the Museum of Fine Arts. On his return to Italy, he traveled in November to Munich, Berlin, Prague, and Paris.

1995 Went in February to Houston for the opening of the second stop of the retrospective, and for the inauguration of the Cy Twombly Gallery at the Menil Collection, sponsored by Philippa and Heiner Friedrich, curated by Paul Winkler. The gallery was designed by Renzo Piano based on plans by Twombly, who worked in close collaboration with the architect. The gallery permanently displays paintings, sculptures, and works on paper from 1954 on. Twombly spent the spring in Lexington, and the summer in Gaeta, where he completed the second version of the set of *Quattro Stagioni*. He traveled to Berlin in August, then to St. Petersburg.

1996 After spending the winter in Lexington, he traveled to Paris in June. In Gaeta during the summer he worked on sculptures and three sets of monoprints, which were shown that fall in New York at the Whitney Museum of American Art. He traveled to Japan in October, to receive the "Premium Imperiale." He spent the winter in Lexington and on St. Barthélemy in the Caribbean.

1997 Spent the winter in St. Barthélemy in the Caribbean, the spring in Lexington, and the summer in Gaeta. In November his first one-artist sculpture exhibition in the United States opened at Gagosian Gallery, New York.

1998 Spent the winter in Lexington, where he concentrated on sculpture.

1999 Exhibited eight sculptures at the American Academy in Rome. In May he traveled to Iran and visited Esfahān. In Gaeta he painted the trilogy *Three Studies from the Temeraire*, for the exhibition *Encounters—New Art from Old* at the National Gallery in London. In August he made sculpture in Bassano. Spent the fall and winter in Lexington.

2000 In March he returned to Rome via Basel, where the retrospective of sixty-six sculptures made between 1946 and 1998 opened in April at the Kunstmuseum. The exhibition, curated by Katharina Schmidt in collaboration with Paul Winkler, was later presented at the Menil Collection in Houston and the National Gallery in Washington, DC. *Coronation of Sesostris* was exhibited at Gagosian Gallery, New York.

2001 During the winter and spring in Lexington, he worked on sculptures, photographs, and the series of *Lepanto* paintings, which were presented at the Venice Biennale, where he was awarded the Leone d'Oro prize. Traveled to the Institut Valencia d'Art Modern, Spain, where he was awarded the Gonzalez Prize. Worked on sculptures during the summer and fall in Gaeta.

2002 Spent the winter in Gaeta and the spring in Lexington, where he devoted his time to sculpture and photography.

2003 Spent the winter months in St. Barthélemy. Returned to Lexington in the spring, where he painted *A Gathering of Time*, which was shown at the Gagosian Gallery in New York in May. Traveled in July to Russia, where, on the occasion of the 300th anniversary of the city of St. Petersburg, the State Hermitage Museum presented *Cy Twombly at the Hermitage Fifty Years of Works on Paper*. The retrospective, which traveled in October to the Staatliche Graphische Sammlung, Pinakothek der Moderne, Munich, was curated by Julie Sylvester. Spent the fall and winter in Gaeta.

2004 *Cy Twombly Fifty Years of Works on Paper* continued its tour to Centre Pompidou, Paris, in January and to the Serpentine Gallery, London, in April. Ten paintings which were completed in Gaeta were shown at the Gagosian Gallery in London in the summer. Returned to Lexington in the fall.

ONE-ARTIST EXHIBITIONS

1951 – Chicago, The Seven Stairs Gallery. *Cy Twombly.* Nov. 2–30.
1953 – Rome, Galleria Via della Croce 71–int. 2, *Arazzi di Cy Twombly.* March 7.
– Princeton, the little gallery. *Cy Twombly. Drawings, Paintings, Sculpture.* Oct. 25–Nov. 7.
1955 – New York, The Stable Gallery. *Cy Twombly.* Jan. 10–29.
1956 – New York, The Stable Gallery. *Cy Twombly.* Jan. 2–19.
1957 – New York, The Stable Gallery. *Cy Twombly.* Jan. 2–19.
1958 – Rome, Galleria La Tartaruga. *Cy Twombly.* Opened May 17.
– Venice, Galleria del Cavallino. *Cy Twombly.* Aug. 18–27.
– Milan, Galleria del Naviglio. *Cy Twombly.* Nov. 1–10.
1960 – Rome, Galleria La Tartaruga. *Cy Twombly.* Opened April 26.
– New York, Leo Castelli Gallery. *Cy Twombly.* Oct. 18–Nov. 5.
1961 – Rome, Galleria La Tartaruga. *Cy Twombly.*
– Milan, Galleria del Naviglio. *Cy Twombly.* March 29–April 7.
– Essen, Galerie Rudolf Zwirner. *Cy Twombly.* Oct.
– Paris, Galerie J. *Cy Twombly, La révolution du signe.* Nov.
1962 – Venice, Galleria del Leone. *Cy Twombly.* Opened June 11.
1963 – Rome, Galleria La Tartaruga. *Twombly.* Opened March 5.
– Cologne, Galerie Rudolf Zwirner. *Cy Twombly.* Opened April 4.
– Cologne, Galerie Änne Abels. *Cy Twombly.* April 20–May 15.
– Turin, Galleria Notizie. *Dipinti di Cy Twombly.* May 14–June 15.
– Geneva, Galerie D. Benador. *Cy Twombly. Peintures, dessins.* Opened Dec. 6.
1964 – Lausanne, Galerie Bonnier. *Cy Twombly. Peintures récentes.* Jan.–Feb. Traveled to:
• Basel, Galerie Handschin. *Cy Twombly.* March 13–April 30.
– New York, Leo Castelli Gallery. *Nine Discourses on Commodus by Cy Twombly.* March 14–April 9.
– Munich, Galerie Friedrich + Dahlem. *Cy Twombly. Notes from a Tower/The Artist in the Northern Climate.* Nov.–Dec.
1965 – Krefeld, Museum Haus Lange. *Cy Twombly.* Oct. 3–Nov. 21. Traveled to:
• Brussels, Palais des Beaux-Arts. Dec. 2–26;
• Amsterdam, Stedelijk Museum. Jan. 14–Feb. 27, 1966.
– Turin, Galleria Notizie. *Cy Twombly.* Opened Oct. 5.
1966 – New York, Leo Castelli Gallery. *Cy Twombly. Drawings.* Feb. 12–March 2.
1967 – Turin, Galleria Notizie. *Cy Twombly.* Opened Feb. 15.
– Rome, Galleria La Tartaruga. *Cy Twombly.* April.
– New York, Leo Castelli Gallery. *Cy Twombly.* Oct. 7–26.
1968 – Milwaukee, Milwaukee Art Center. *Cy Twombly. Paintings and Drawings.* Jan. 19–Feb. 18.
– Rome, Galleria La Tartaruga. *Disegni e collages di Cy Twombly 1954–1968.* Opened Feb. 26.
– Cologne, Galerie Hake. *Cy Twombly. Zeichnungen.* Nov. 27–Dec. 21.
– New York, Leo Castelli Gallery. *Cy Twombly. Paintings.* Nov. 30–Dec. 21.
– Los Angeles, Nicholas Wilder Gallery. *Cy Twombly. Recent Paintings.*
1969 – Cologne, Galerie Rudolf Zwirner. *Cy Twombly.* Jan.–Feb.
1970 – Rome, La Tartaruga, Studio d'Arte. *Cy Twombly, una mostra di opere recenti.* Opened Feb. 28.
– Stockholm, Svensk-Franska Konstgalleriet. *Cy Twombly. Paintings.* March 1–April 10.
– Cologne, Galerie Neuendorf. *Cy Twombly. "Roman Notes." 24 neue Arbeiten.* April 22–May 20.
– Frankfurt, Galerie Ursula Lichter. *Cy Twombly.* May 27–June 20.
– Geneva, Galerie Bonnier. *Cy Twombly. Peintures, dessins, lithographies.* June 4–30.
1971 – Turin, Galleria Sperone. *Cy Twombly.* Opened Feb. 22.
– Cologne, Galerie Möllenhoff. *Cy Twombly. Bilder, Zeichnungen.* May 3–24.
– Paris, Galerie Yvon Lambert. *Cy Twombly.* Opened June 10.
– Düsseldorf, Galerie Denise René/Hans Mayer, Kunstmarkt für Grafik und Objekte. *Cy Twombly. 8 Gouachen aus dem Jahr 1971.* Sept.
– Berlin, Galerie Folker Skulima. *Cy Twombly. 8 Gouachen 1971.* Sept.
– Milan, Galleria dell'Ariete. *Cy Twombly.* Opened Oct. 7.
1972 – Toronto, Dunkelman Gallery. *Cy Twombly. Paintings and Works on Paper.*
– New York, Leo Castelli Gallery. *Cy Twombly.* Jan. 15–Feb. 5.
– Milan, Galleria dell'Ariete. *Cy Twombly.* April.
– Rome, Galleria dell'Oca. *Disegni di Cy Twombly dal 1960–1965.* Opened May 26.
– Dallas, Janie C. Lee Gallery. *Cy Twombly.* Opened April 22.
– Naples, Lucio Amelio—Modern Art Agency. *Cy Twombly. Ramifications.* Opened Nov. 18.
– Minneapolis, Locksley-Shea Gallery. *Cy Twombly.* Opened Dec. 2.
1973 – Turin, Galleria Gian Enzo Sperone. *Cy Twombly.* Jan. 8–29.
– New York, Visual Arts Museum. *Cy Twombly. Drawings.* Jan. 11–Feb. 6.
– Zurich, Galerie Art in Progress. *Cy Twombly. Bilder, Zeichnungen, Grafiken.* Feb. 23–March 22.
– Bern, Kunsthalle. *Cy Twombly. Bilder 1953–1972.* April 28–June 3. Traveled to:
• Munich, Städtische Galerie im Lenbachhaus. July 10–Aug. 12.
– Basel, Kunstmuseum. *Cy Twombly, Zeichnungen 1953–1973.* May 5–June 24.
– London, The Mayor Gallery. *Cy Twombly.* May 16–June 9.
1974 – Munich, Galerie Heiner Friedrich. *Cy Twombly. Roman Notes, Gouachen 1970.* March 7–April 7.
– Turin, Galleria Gian Enzo Sperone. *Cy Twombly.* Opened March 12.
– Brussels, Galerie Oppenheim. *Cy Twombly.* April 2–27.
– Paris, Galerie Yvon Lambert. *Cy Twombly.* April 18–May 14.
– Naples, Lucio Amelio—Modern Art Agency. *Cy Twombly, Portfolio tecnica mista, collage, disegno, Natural History, Part I.* Dec. 13, 1974–Jan. 10, 1975.
1975 – Berlin, Galerie Georg Nothelfer. *Cy Twombly—graphic-works.* Jan. 17–Feb. 27.
– Geneva, Galerie Jacques Benador. *Cy Twombly. Dessins.* Feb.
– Naples, Lucio Amelio—Modern Art Agency. *Cy Twombly. Allusions (Bay of Naples).* Feb. 21–March 21.
– Cologne, Galerie Karsten Greve. *Cy Twombly. Bilder und Zeichnungen.* March 1–April 15.
– Munich, Galerie Art in Progress. *Cy Twombly—Graue Bilder und Gouachen.* March 7–April 15.
– Philadelphia, Institute of Contemporary Art, University of Pennsylvania. *Cy Twombly. Paintings, Drawings, Constructions 1951–1974.* March 15–April 27. Traveled to:
• San Francisco, San Francisco Museum of Art. May 9–June 22.
– Munich, Galerie des Verlages Schellmann & Klüser. *Cy Twombly. Graphische Zyklen.* Oct. 2–30.

1976 – Düsseldorf, Galerie Art in Progress. *Cy Twombly. Bilder und Gouachen.* Jan. 30–March 4.
– Hannover, Kestner-Gesellschaft. *Cy Twombly.* May 7–June 20.
– Paris, Galerie Jacques Bosser. *Cy Twombly. Editions récentes.* June 22–Sept. 30.
– Paris, Musée d'art moderne de la Ville de Paris, ARC 2. *Cy Twombly, Dessins 1954–1976.* June 24–Sept. 6.
– Munich, Galerie Schellmann & Klüser. *Cy Twombly. Six Latin Writers and Poets. Some Trees of Italy.* Sept. 1–30.
– New York, Leo Castelli Gallery. *Cy Twombly. Watercolors.* Sept. 25–Oct. 16.
– Rome, Galleria Gian Enzo Sperone. *Cy Twombly.* Nov. 23–Dec. 17.

1977 – Karlsruhe, Galerie Haus 11. *Cy Twombly.* Jan. 21–March 5.
– New York, Visual Arts Museum. *Cy Twombly: Paintings.* March 8–30.
– Paris, Galerie Yvon Lambert. *Cy Twombly. Three Dialogues.* May 17–June 15.
– Cologne, Galerie Karsten Greve. *Cy Twombly. Bilder und Zeichnungen.* May 20–July 15.

1978 – The Hague, Artline. *Cy Twombly.* Jan. 1–Feb. 6.
– Munich, Galerie Klewan. *Cy Twombly. Bilder, Collagen, Zeichnungen.* March 2–31.
– New York, The Lone Star Foundation at Heiner Friedrich, Inc. *Cy Twombly. 50 Days at Iliam.* Nov. 18, 1978–Jan. 20, 1979.

1979 – New York, Whitney Museum of American Art. *Cy Twombly. Paintings and Drawings 1954–1977.* April 10–June 10.
– Naples, Galleria Lucio Amelio. Cy *Twombly. 11 sculture.* Opened May 25.
– Lund, Galleriet. *12 lithografier av Cy Twombly.* Sept. 29–Oct. 24.
– Cologne, Galerie Karsten Greve. *Cy Twombly. Bilder 1957–1968.* Nov. 6, 1979–Jan. 20, 1980.

1980 – Dallas, The University Gallery, Meadows School of the Arts, Southern Methodist University. *Cy Twombly. Paintings and Drawings.* Jan. 15–Feb. 26.
– London, The Mayor Gallery. *Cy Twombly. Paintings and Drawings 1959–1976.* March 18–April 19.
– Spoleto, Palazzo Ancaiani, 23° Festival dei Due Mondi. *Cy Twombly. Disegni 1955–1975.* June 26–July 13.
– Seattle, Richard Hines Gallery. Cy *Twombly. Paintings & Drawings 1956–1975.* July 24–Aug. 30.
– Milan, Padiglione d'Arte Contemporanea. *Cy Twombly. 50 disegni 1953–1980.* Oct.–Nov.
– Hamburg, Galerie Munro. *Cy Twombly. Malerei—Zeichnung—Grafik.* Oct. 9–Dec. 20.
– Paris, Galerie Yvon Lambert. *Cy Twombly.* Oct. 18–Nov. 20.
– Madrid, Galeria Heinrich Ehrhardt. *Cy Twombly. Dibujos.* Dec. 15, 1980–Feb. 15, 1981.

1981 – New York, Castelli Graphics. *Cy Twombly. Natural History. Part I: Some Trees of Italy, Part II: Mushrooms.* June 6–27.
– Krefeld, Museum Haus Lange. *Cy Twombly. Skulpturen. 23 Arbeiten aus den Jahren 1955 bis 1981.* Sept. 27–Nov. 15.
– Newport Beach, Harbor Art Museum. *Cy Twombly. Works on Paper 1954–1976.* Oct. 2–Nov. 29. Traveled to:
  • Madison, Elvehjem Museum of Art. Jan. 24–March 18, 1982;
  • Richmond, Virginia Museum of Fine Arts. June 15–July 18, 1982;
  • Toronto, Art Gallery of Ontario. Sept. 4–Oct. 17, 1982.
– Lund, Galleriet. *Cy Twombly. Natural History. Part I: Some Trees of Italy, Part II: Mushrooms.* Oct. 31–Nov. 25.

1982 – New York, Sperone Westwater Fischer. *Cy Twombly. XI Recent Works.* April 1–May 8.
– Rome, Il Ponte. *Cy Twombly, opere su carta.* Opened April 22.
– Cologne, Galerie Karsten Greve. *Cy Twombly. Arbeiten auf Papier.* June 4–July 31.
– London, The Mayor Gallery. *Cy Twombly. An Exhibition of Paintings.* Sept. 28–Nov. 6.
– Paris, Galerie Yvon Lambert. *Cy Twombly.* Oct. 16–Nov. 18.
– Vancouver, The Vancouver Art Gallery. *Cy Twombly: Prints.* Dec. 11, 1982–Jan. 30, 1983.

1983 – New York, Stephen Mazoh Gallery. *Cy Twombly. Paintings.* April 19–May 27.

1984 – Cologne, Galerie Karsten Greve. *Cy Twombly.* Jan. 27–March 25. Traveled to:
  • London, The Mayor Gallery. April 2–May 4;
  • Vienna, Galerie Ulysses. May 24–June 23.
– Naples, Galleria Lucio Amelio. *Cy Twombly.* Opened Feb. 8.
– Bordeaux, capc Musée d'art contemporain. *Cy Twombly. Œuvres de 1973–1983.* May 19–Sept. 9.
– Baden-Baden, Staatliche Kunsthalle. *Cy Twombly.* Sept. 23–Nov. 11.
– New York, Hirschl & Adler Modern. *Cy Twombly. Paintings and Drawings: 1952–1984.* Oct. 11–Nov. 3.
– Rome, Galleria Gian Enzo Sperone. *Cy Twombly. Sculture.* Opened Oct. 25.

1985 – New York, Dia Art Foundation. *Cy Twombly. Paintings and Drawings.* Oct. 31, 1985–March 15, 1986.
– Cologne, Galerie Karsten Greve. *Cy Twombly.* Nov. 16, 1985–Jan. 8, 1986.
– Zurich, Galerie & Edition Stähli. *Cy Twombly. Drawings and Prints.* Nov. 23, 1985–Jan. 18, 1986.

1986 – Paris, Opéra Bastille. *Rideau de Scène* for the theater.
– New York, Gagosian Gallery. *Cy Twombly. Drawings, Collages, and Paintings on Paper: 1955–1985.* Feb. 22–April 5.
– New York, Hirschl & Adler Modern. *Cy Twombly.* April 12–May 7.
– Cologne, Galerie Karsten Greve. *Cy Twombly. Paintings.* Sept. 2–Nov. 6.

1987 – Zurich, Kunsthaus. *Cy Twombly. Bilder, Arbeiten auf Papier, Skulpturen.* Feb. 18–March 29. Traveled to:
  • Madrid, Palacio de Velázquez/Palacio de Cristal. *Cy Twombly. Cuadros, trabajos sobre papel, esculturas.* April 22–July 30;
  • London, Whitechapel Art Gallery. *Cy Twombly. Paintings, Works on Paper, Sculpture.* Sept. 25–Nov. 15;
  • Düsseldorf, Städtische Kunsthalle. *Cy Twombly. Bilder, Arbeiten auf Papier, Skulpturen.* Dec. 11, 1987–Jan. 31, 1988;
  • Paris, Musée national d'art moderne, Galeries contemporaines, Centre Georges Pompidou. *Cy Twombly. Peintures, Œuvres sur papier, Sculptures.* Feb. 16–April 17, 1988;
– Genoa, Galleria La Polena. *Cy Twombly, Natural History, Part II, Trees.* Feb. 26.
– Bonn, Städtisches Kunstmuseum. *Cy Twombly. Serien auf Papier 1957–1987.* June 2–Aug. 9. Traveled to:
  • Barcelona, Centre Cultural de la Fundació Caixa de Pensions. *Cy Twombly. Sèries sobre papel 1959–1987.* Nov. 30, 1987–Jan. 17, 1988.
– Siegen, Städtische Galerie Haus Seel. *Cy Twombly.* June 28–Aug. 2.
– London, Anthony d'Offay Gallery. *Cy Twombly. Paintings and Works on Paper and the North African Sketchbook 1953.* Sept. 26–Oct. 31.

1988 – New York, The Pace Gallery. *Cy Twombly. Works on Paper.* Jan. 8–30.
– Munich, Galerie Klewan. *Cy Twombly. Grafik der Siebzigerjahre.* Feb. 4–March 31.
– Bridgehampton, Dia Art Foundation. *Cy Twombly. Poems to the Sea.* May 28–June 30.
– New York, Vrej Baghoomian, Inc. *Cy Twombly.* Sept. 24–Oct. 22.
– St. Louis, The Greenberg Gallery. *Cy Twombly. Works on Paper.* Oct. 7–Nov. 12.

1989 – New York, Sperone Westwater. *Cy Twombly. Paintings and Sculptures 1951 and 1953.* Feb. 1–28.
– Cologne, Galerie Karsten Greve. *Paintings of Cy Twombly.* Spring.
– Houston, The Menil Collection. *Cy Twombly.* Sept. 8, 1989–March 4, 1990. Traveled to:
• Des Moines, Des Moines Art Center. April 28–June 17, 1990.
– Paris, Galerie Di Meo. *Twombly.* Sept. 29–Dec. 23.
– New York, Gagosian Gallery. *Cy Twombly. Bolsena.* Dec. 12, 1989–Jan. 20, 1990.
1990 – Zurich, Thomas Ammann Fine Art. *Cy Twombly. Drawings and 8 Sculptures.* June 11–Sept. 1.
– Paris, Ameliobrachot/Pièce Unique. *Cy Twombly. Summer Madness.* Oct. 23–Nov. 24.
1991 – Paris, Ameliobrachot/Pièce Unique. *Cy Twombly. Thermopylae.* Oct. 2–Dec. 20.
– New York, Hirschl & Adler Modern. *Cy Twombly. Prints 1952–1983.* Nov. 21, 1991–Jan. 4, 1992.
1992 – Paris, Galerie Vidal—Saint Phalle. *Cy Twombly—œuvres gravées.* Sept. 12–Nov. 4.
1993 – Paris, Galerie Karsten Greve. *Cy Twombly. Peintures, Œuvres sur papier et Sculptures.* May 29–Oct. 20.
– Paris, Pièce Unique. *Cy Twombly.* Oct. 2–Nov. 30.
– New York, Matthew Marks Gallery. *Cy Twombly. Photographs.* Oct. 15–Dec. 4.
– Bonn, Kunstmuseum Bonn. *Cy Twombly—Octavio Paz.* Nov. 5, 1993–Jan. 9, 1994.
1994 – Milan, Galleria Karsten Greve. *Cy Twombly.* April 9–May 25.
– Zurich, Thomas Ammann Fine Art. *Cy Twombly.* June 15–Sept. 15.
– New York, The Museum of Modern Art. *Cy Twombly. A Retrospective.* Sept. 21, 1994–Jan. 10, 1995. Traveled to:
• Houston, The Menil Collection. Feb. 12–March 19, 1995;
• Los Angeles, The Museum of Contemporary Art. April 9–June 11, 1995;
• Berlin, Neue Nationalgalerie. *Cy Twombly. Retrospektive.* Aug. 31–Nov. 19, 1995.
– New York, Gagosian Gallery. *Cy Twombly. Untitled Painting, "Say Goodbye Catullus to the Shores of Asia Minor."* Sept. 24, 1994–Jan. 7, 1995.
– New York, C & M Arts (in association with Galerie Karsten Greve, Cologne/Paris/Milan). *Cy Twombly.* Sept. 27–Nov. 12.
1995 – Houston, The Museum of Fine Arts. *Cy Twombly. Untitled Painting, "Say Goodbye Catullus to the Shores of Asia Minor."* Feb. 4–19.
– Houston, Texas Gallery. *Cy Twombly. Photographs.* Feb. 8–March 25.
– Houston, Robert McClain & Co. *Cy Twombly: Works on Paper from Four Decades.* Feb. 9–March 11.
– Goslar, Mönchehaus—Museum für Moderne Kunst. *Cy Twombly, prints.* May 11–June 29.
– Berlin, Galerie Max Hetzler. *Cy Twombly. Skulptur.* June 3–July 22.
1996 – New York, Peder Bonnier Gallery. *Cy Twombly.* May 2–June 1.
– Los Angeles, Gagosian Gallery. *Cy Twombly. Photographs.* May 11–June 29.
– Salzburg, Rupertinum. *Cy Twombly, Drawings and Lithos.* May 18–July 7.
– São Paolo, *23 Bienal Internacional São Paulo, Sals epeciais.* Oct. 5–Dec. 8.
– New York, Whitney Museum of American Art. *Cy Twombly. Lepanto* (three cardboard plate engravings printed as mono-prints). Dec. 2.
1997 – Rome, Galleria S.A.L.E.S. *Cy Twombly. Photographs.* June 6–Summer.
– Cologne, Galerie Karsten Greve. *Cy Twombly.* June 25–Sept.
– New York, Gagosian Gallery. *Cy Twombly. Sculpture.* Opened Nov. 5.
1998 – Rome, American Academy. *Cy Twombly. Eight Sculptures.* Sept. 29–Nov. 15.
2000 – Basel, Kunstmuseum Basel. *Cy Twombly. The Sculpture.* April 15–July 30.
– Houston, The Menil Collection. *Cy Twombly. The Sculpture.* Sept. 20–Jan. 7, 2001.
– New York, Gagosian Gallery. *Cy Twombly. Coronation of Sesostris.* Nov. 11–Jan. 27, 2001.
2001 – Washington, DC, National Gallery of Art. *Cy Twombly: The Sculpture.* May 6–July 29.
– Zurich, Thomas Ammann Fine Art. *Cy Twombly. 6 Paintings 3 Sculptures.* June 11–Sept. 28.
2002 – New York, Gagosian Gallery. *Cy Twombly. Lepanto.* Jan. 19–Feb. 16.
– Zurich, Daros Exhibitions, *Audible Silence: Cy Twombly at Daros.* May 3–Sept. 7.
– Edinburgh, Inverleith House, Royal Botanic Garden. *Cy Twombly.* Aug. 9–Oct. 27.
– Munich, Alte Pinakothek. *Cy Twombly. Lepanto.* Sept. 4–Nov. 24.
– Munich, Schirmer/Mosel Showroom. *Cy Twombly: Photographs 2002.* Sept. 6–Oct. 22.
– Cagliari, EXMA Centro dell'Arte e Cultura, *Twombly. Sculpture.* Nov. 6–Dec. 8.
2003 – New York, Gagosian Gallery. *Cy Twombly. A Gathering of Time.* May 12–July 12.
– St. Petersburg, The State Hermitage Museum. *Cy Twombly at the Hermitage Fifty Years of Works on Paper.* July 8–Sept. 21.
– Munich, Staatliche Graphische Sammlung, Pinakothek der Moderne. *Cy Twombly Fifty Years of Works on Paper.* Oct. 8–Nov. 30.
2004 – Paris, Musée National d'Art Moderne, Centre Pompidou. *Cy Twombly Fifty Years of Works on Paper.* Jan. 21–March 29.
– London, The Serpentine Gallery. *Cy Twombly Fifty Years of Works on Paper.* April 17–June 13.
– London, Gagosian Gallery. *Ten Paintings and a Sculpture.* May 27–July 31.

MONOGRAPHS

1961 – Galleria La Tartaruga. *Cy Twombly.* Rome. Text by Emilio Villa.

1970 – Stocchi, Gabriele. addenda ed. *Cy Twombly. 11 Grey Paintings 1967–1970.* Rome. One hundred examples signed and numbered by the artist. With etching.

1973 – Bastian, Heiner. *Cy Twombly. Zeichnungen 1953–1973.* Frankfurt/Main, Berlin, and Vienna.

1978 – Bastian, Heiner. *Cy Twombly. Bilder/Paintings 1952–1976.* Frankfurt/Main, Berlin, and Vienna.

1979 – Lambert, Yvon. *Catalogue raisonné des œuvres sur papier de Cy Twombly, Volume VI 1973–1976.* Milan. Text by Roland Barthes, "Non multa sed multum."
– Bastian, Heiner. *Cy Twombly. Fifty Days at Iliam. A Painting in Ten Parts.* Frankfurt/Main, Berlin, and Vienna. (See also 1990: 2d ed., Stuttgart.)

1981 – Stocchi, Gabriele. addenda ed. *5 Days Wait at Jiayuguan.* Rome. One hundred examples signed and numbered by the artist.

1983 – Barthes, Roland. *Cy Twombly.* Berlin. ("Non multa sed multum" first published in Milan, 1979, and by the Whitney Museum of American Art, New York, 1979.)

1985 – Bastian, Heiner. *Cy Twombly. Das graphische Werk 1953–1984. A Catalogue Raisonné of the Printed Graphic Work.* Munich. Text by Heiner Bastian, "Weil es nicht sein darf, weil es geschieht." (English ed. published by New York University Press, New York.)
– *The Shepheardes Calendar* by Edmund Spenser. Illustrated by Cy Twombly. London.

1986 – Heyden, Thomas. *Zu sehen und zu lesen. Anmerkungen zum Verständnis des Geschriebenen bei Cy Twombly.* Nuremberg.

1987 – Hine Editions. *Cy Twombly. Gaeta Sets.* San Francisco.

1989 – Bastian, Heiner. *Cy Twombly. 24 Short Pieces.* Munich. Text by Heiner Bastian, "Bemerkungen/Comments."

1990 – Bastian, Heiner. *Cy Twombly. Poems to the Sea.* Munich. Text by Heiner Bastian.
– Bastian, Heiner. *Cy Twombly. Fifty Days at Iliam. A Painting in Ten Parts.* 2d ed. Stuttgart. (See 1979.)

1991 – Lambert, Yvon. *Catalogue raisonné des œuvres sur papier de Cy Twombly, Volume VII, 1977–1982.* Milan. Text by Philippe Sollers, "Les épiphanies de Twombly."
– Bastian, Heiner. *Cy Twombly. Letter of Resignation.* Munich. Text by Heiner Bastian, "Semina Motuum."

1992 – Ammann, Thomas, ed. *Cy Twombly. Souvenirs of d'Arros and Gaeta.* Zurich.
– Bastian, Heiner. *Cy Twombly. Catalogue Raisonné of the Paintings, Volume I, 1948–1960.* Munich.

1993 – Bastian, Heiner. *Cy Twombly. Catalogue Raisonné of the Paintings, Volume II, 1961–1965.* Munich.
– Bovelet, Jeannette. *Cy Twombly—Naturerfahrung in der Moderne.* Essen.
– Brandhorst, Udo, ed. *Octavio Paz—Cy Twombly.* Cologne.

1994 – Bastian, Heiner. *Cy Twombly. Catalogue Raisonné of the Paintings, Volume III, 1966–1971.* Munich.

1995 – Bastian, Heiner. *Cy Twombly. Catalogue Raisonné of the Paintings, Volume IV, 1972–1995.* Munich.
– Göricke, Jutta. *Cy Twombly—Spurensuche, München Silke Schreiber Verlag.* Munich.

1997 – Del Roscio, Nicola, ed. *Cy Twombly: Catalogue Raisonné of Sculpture, Volume I 1946–1977.* Munich.
– Sylvester, David. *Cy Twombly: Ten Sculptures.* New York.
– Damisch, Hubert, and Schwemmer, Oswald. *Cy Twombly.* Cologne.

1998 – American Academy in Rome. *Cy Twombly, Eight Sculptures.* Rome.

2000 – Schmidt, Katharina. *Cy Twombly: the Sculpture.* Basel.
– Shapiro, David. *Cy Twombly Coronation of Sesostris.* New York. Poems by David Shapiro and Patricia Waters.

2001 – Frei, Georg. *Cy Twombly 6 Paintings 3 Sculptures.* Zurich.

2002 – Howard, Richard, and Kirk Varnedoe. *Cy Twombly: Lepanto.* New York.
– Keller, Eva, and Regula Malin, eds. *Audible Silence: Cy Twombly at Daros.* Zurich. With contributions by Heiner Bastian.
– Francis, Mark. *Cy Twombly at Inverleith House Royal Botanic Garden, Edinburgh.* Edinburgh.
– Hochdörfer, Achim. *Twombly Sculpture.* Nuoro. Introduction by Ugo Collu.
– Katz, Vincent. *Cy Twombly Photographs 1951–1999.* Munich.

2003 – Norden, Linda. *Cy Twombly: A Gathering of Time: Six Paintings and a Sculpture.* New York.
– Schama, Simon, and Sylvester, Julie. *Cy Twombly at the Hermitage Fifty Years of Works on Paper.* St. Petersburg and Munich. (See also 2004: Paris; and 2004: London.)

2004 – Schama, Simon, and Storsve, Jonas. *Cy Twombly Fifty Years of Works on Paper.* Paris.
– Schama, Simon, and Sylvester, Julie. *Cy Twombly at the Hermitage Fifty Years of Works on Paper.* London.
– Leeman, Richard. *Painting, Drawing, Writing (Peintre, Dessiner, Ecrire).* Paris.

This revised and expanded edition of the catalogue
Cy Twombly at the Hermitage: Fifty Years of Works on Paper
was published on the occasion of the exhibition
Cy Twombly: Fifty Years of Works on Paper
at the Whitney Museum of American Art, New York, January 27–May 8, 2005.
The exhibition was curated by Julie Sylvester, Associate Curator of Contemporary Art, The State Hermitage Museum, St. Petersburg.
For the presentation of the exhibition at the Whitney Museum of American Art, Dana Miller, Associate Curator, and Jennifer Goldstein, Curatorial Assistant, lent their assistance.

The State Hermitage Museum Organizing Committee:

Mikhail B. Piotrovsky
Director of The State Hermitage Museum, Doctor of History, Member of the Russian Academy of Science, Member of the Russian Academy of Arts, Professor of Saint Petersburg State University

George V. Vilinbakhov
Deputy Director for Research, Ph.D.

Vladimir U. Matveyev
Deputy Director for Exhibitions and Developments, Ph.D.

Irina N. Novoselskaya
Head of the Western European Art Department, Doctor of Art

Mikhail O. Dedinkin
Senior Researcher of the Western European Art Department

Julie Sylvester
Associate Curator of Contemporary Art

Exhibition Itinerary:

Cy Twombly at the Hermitage
The State Hermitage Museum, St. Petersburg
July 8–September 21, 2003
300th Anniversary of St. Petersburg

Staatliche Graphische Sammlung, Pinakothek der Moderne, Munich
October 7–November 21, 2003

Centre Georges Pompidou, Paris
January 21–March 28, 2004

The Serpentine Gallery, London
April 13–May 23, 2004

Cy Twombly: Fifty Years of Works on Paper
Whitney Museum of American Art, New York
January 27–May 8, 2005

The Menil Collection, Houston
May 27–September 4, 2005

Julie Sylvester wishes to thank, for their great collaboration, Michael Semff of the Staatliche Graphische Sammlung, Munich; Alfred Pacquement and Jonas Storsve of Centre Pompidou, Paris; and Julia Peyton-Jones and Rochelle Steiner of the Serpentine Gallery, London, the last stop of the European tour, where the natural light of the galleries revealed with splendor the truth and freshness of the drawings.

Unless otherwise noted, all photographs are by Mimmo Capone, Hyjdla Kosaniuk, Prudence Cuming Associates

Printed and bound in Germany

Distributed in the United States and Canada by
D. A. P. Distributed Art Publishers, New York

Publications and New Media Department at the Whitney Museum of American Art, New York: Rachel de W. Wixom: head of publications; Thea Hetzner: associate editor; Jennifer MacNair: associate editor, Makiko Ushiba: manager, graphic design; Vickie Leung: production manager; Anita Duquette: manager, rights and reproductions; Arianne Gelardin: publications assistant; Anna Knoell, design assistant.

Major support for this exhibition was provided by Neil G. Bluhm.
Significant funding was provided by The Horace W. Goldsmith Foundation.
Additional support was provided by John Bowes.

Library of Congress Cataloging-in-Publication Data

Twombly, Cy, 1928–
Cy Twombly, fifty years of works on paper.— Rev. ed.
p. cm.
Revised ed. of: Cy Twombly at the Hermitage: fifty years of works on paper.
"Catalog of an exhibition at the Whitney Museum of American Art, New York, Jan. 27–May 8, 2005.
Includes bibliographical references.
ISBN 0-87427-146-0 (pbk. : alk. paper) — ISBN 1-933045-17-5 (hardcover : alk. paper)
1. Twombly, Cy, 1928—Exhibitions. 2. Drawing, Abstract—United States—Exhibitions. I. Title: Cy Twombly. II. Title: Fifty years of works on paper. III. Twombly, Cy, 1928– Cy Twombly at the Hermitage. IV. Whitney Museum of American Art. V. Title.
NC139.T86A4 2005
760'.092—dc22

2004022133